The Lost Lyra

Richard Clark

Praise for Richard Clark's Books

'Clark is particularly good on the colours, flavours and scents of Greece. He has got under the skin of the place in a way few outsiders have been able to.'

Mark Hudson, winner of *Somerset Maugham Award, Thomas Cook Travel Book Award, Samuel Johnson Prize*

'Richard Clark captures the spirit of Greece I love. His books make me long to see the places he describes.'

Jennifer Barclay, author of *Falling in Honey* and *An Octopus in My Ouzo*

'There is poetry in Richard Clark's words and through his eyes. I recommend anyone missing Greece, visiting Greece or just wishing they could go to Greece to take a look!'

Sara Alexi, author of *The Greek Village Series*

'Thanks, Richard, for adding your great eye to your gifted pen in service to sharing the essence of Greece with the world!'

Jeffrey Siger, award-winning US crime writer

'Richard Clark writes with great authority and a deep affection for his subject, which comes from his long association with Greece… excellent.'

Marjory McGinn, author of *Things Can Only Get Feta, Homer's Where the Heart Is, A Scorpion in the Lemon Tree* and *A Saint for the Summer*

By the Same Author

The Greek Islands – A Notebook

Crete – A Notebook

Rhodes – A Notebook

Corfu – A Notebook

Hidden Crete – A Notebook

More Hidden Crete – A Notebook

Eastern Crete – A Notebook

Richard Clark's Greek Islands Anthology

The Crete Trilogy

The Lost Lyra

First published in Great Britain and the USA 2019

Copyright © Richard Clark 2019

Cover design © Mike Parsons 2019

ISBN – 978-1791579432

www.facebook.com/richardclarkbooks

https://notesfromgreece.com

About the Author

Richard Clark is a writer, editor and journalist who has worked on an array of national newspapers and magazines in the UK. In 1982, on a whim, he decided to up sticks and live on the Greek island of Crete. So began a love affair that has continued to this day, and he still visits the Greek islands, where he has a home, on a regular basis. In 2016, he gave up the daily commute to London to become a full-time author. He is married with two grown up children and two grandchildren, and lives in Kent.

Acknowledgements

This book is a work of fiction, although the story is informed by the real and tragic events in Crete during the years of the Second World War. Any mistakes are mine alone.

Since I set out on the journey to be an author I have had so much help and support from many people; you know who you are – thank you.

I owe a debt of gratitude to Tony and Bernadette Prouse for generously agreeing to read the book as it came to fruition and for suggesting many ways it could be improved. Similarly, a massive thank you to Mark Hudson, Yvonne Payne, Kay Rodgers and David Harding for reading my first draft and being such rigorous, helpful and supportive critics.

This book could not have made it onto the shelf without the exacting editing skills of Jennifer Barclay and the beautiful cover design of Mike Parsons, to them I give my grateful thanks. I also owe much to the many friends and neighbours in Crete who have never ceased to make me feel welcome. My last thank you goes to my family, Denise, Rebecca, James, Lucy, Pete, Esther and Imogen who have been with me on the journey.

Note

The names of male Greek characters ending in an 's' will drop the letter in the vocative case (when that character is being addressed in direct speech).

This book is a work of fiction. All the characters, names and events are the product of the author's imagination and any resemblance to real persons, living or dead, is purely coincidental.

For Denise

Chapter 1

THE SIGHT OF the austere cross jolted her, throwing her back to that day three weeks previously which had led her to this place. Her emotions had been as raw that day as these parched hills and as confused as the intimidating streets she had walked today from the coast to arrive on top of the city walls. In her old life, the cacophony of the island's unruly capital would have fired her imagination with possibilities. Today they fed her anxiety. Any scintilla of confidence that remained had drained away as the sights and sounds of the city lay siege to her senses.

Exhausted from a sleepless overnight ferry crossing spent on deck, after disembarking, Sarah had just kept walking, trying to escape the hawkers of rooms to rent, meals to eat or tat to buy. She needed somewhere silent to collect her thoughts: perhaps not here?

It was certainly quiet, a relief from the bustle of the dusty streets and alleys of the city below but the austere wooden cross reminded her of the temporary memorial placed at the head of her grandfather's newly dug grave back in England.

Three weeks ago the spring heavens had opened to receive Sarah's grandfather and deluge the gathered mourners collected beside his muddy, open grave. Beneath a dripping umbrella held by a coated, sombre undertaker the priest had scattered earth, ashes and dust on the dank coffin.

Little more than three weeks ago, Sarah was living a life charted in her chosen direction. Now those plans lay as dead as the man she had cherished for most of her life.

Dishevelled and drained, her thoughts found her alone in the world, in a strange country, friendless and with nowhere to stay. Atop those stern walls, the sun beat remorselessly, but could not stem the flood of panic that threatened to overwhelm her.

Sarah lowered a holdall and two hard cases, of the sort used to carry musical instruments, to the scrubby ground. Now sitting, she surveyed the view over terracotta roof tiles of traditional homes rubbing up against the sparkling white concrete of apartment blocks, offices and shops. Criss-crossed steel trunks of cranes and a jumble of TV aerials peeped over the escarpment, punctuating an urban sprawl mitigated by the backdrop of an ultramarine sea stretching to infinity.

For a moment, she closed her eyes. The warmth of the sun washed over her. Then a glimmer of the clarity she so needed was destroyed by voices. A tour party gathered around a guide holding an umbrella. They did not notice the tousled, petite young Englishwoman, her long dark hair shadowing green eyes rendered shallow by exhaustion as she sat surrounded by her luggage.

The moment gone, Sarah couldn't tune out of the well-worn spiel which, after a few sentences, emerged as English. Drawn in by the guide, despite herself, she heard him explain that this was the grave of Greece's greatest modern writer who died 54 years ago, Nikos Kazantzakis. Although this meant nothing to Sarah there was a hint of recognition when *Zorba the Greek* was mentioned. Apparently, 'following his death in 1957, Nikos was laid to rest here on top of the walls which encircle Heraklion, the city he so loved as, excommunicated by the Orthodox Church, he was buried in unconsecrated ground… The plaque upon the grave has the epitaph "I hope for nothing. I fear nothing. I am free."'

Something in these words spoke directly to Sarah, striking a chord with those in the note her granddad had left her. Eager to return to their cruise ship the tourists disinterestedly moved away. Sarah edged towards the grave. Just then, under that unrelenting sun, the mists of her insecurities began to clear.

She returned to her meagre luggage and sat to contemplate her next move. This in itself was progress; she was at least looking to

3

the future. First things first; find a place to stay, somewhere to gather her thoughts, regroup, and take up the plan so hastily made in the eye of the storm of her grief and anger. At the time, leaving England had seemed a good idea, a way of escaping, giving herself space to make sense of everything.

Athens astern, the ferry forged forward, drawing a white wake across the azure water. The sun turned golden then sank, the disappearing lights of Athens riding the waves like a giant cruise liner. The blue-black sky was ablaze with stars. Occasionally a cluster of lights from some small island would appear like a mystical galaxy adrift on a watery universe.

As night deepened, fellow passengers drifted off to their cabins below or bedded down to sleep on deck. Unable to sleep, the tiredness that gripped her had wrung her out by the time the ship found its dawn landfall in Heraklion.

Her overloaded senses were numb to the cries of traders selling all manner of fruit, vegetables, meat, fish, herbs and spices. The rising heat of the day playing on her fragile confidence she headed uphill, away from the madness of the town centre, until the southern boundary of the city walls barred her way.

Here at least she had found space to take one step forward and determined to find herself a place to stay. Calmer, she descended the stone steps, leaving the writer's grave behind but carrying in her head the inscription. Re-entering the hubbub of the city, in the back streets of the town near a small green park celebrating Heraklion's most famous painter, El Greco, she found a pension with a first-floor room opening onto a small balcony that looked down on the street.

Dumping her holdall on the single rushwork chair and her instrument cases on the bed, she flung open the window then headed for the shower. The modest trickle of water proved adequate to wash away the dust of her journey and taking a moment to lie down on the bed she succumbed to sleep.

On awakening, she saw the sun was low and found a cool welcome as she stepped out onto the balcony festooned with pots of geraniums. Sleep had restored her equilibrium and she was ready to find something to eat and make plans for what to do next.Three weeks before, it had taken all Sarah's composure to stand and read the eulogy at her grandfather's funeral. The priest had held out a hand of comfort as he saw her struggle but she turned away, closed her eyes and somehow found the resolve to continue. Despite the events of that morning, she owed it to her grandfather's memory to remain strong. He had meant everything to her, without his love and guidance, her life could have been so different.

In the car that followed the hearse, Sarah had never felt so alone. The storm that had broken during the service imitating the tears she finally let fall and the internal turmoil that wrenched at her guts. As the cortege swung into the graveyard, Sarah found some slither of strength to recover her poise and lead the mourners to the brink of the empty grave.

She had been her grandfather's only existing family, though he was popular with his neighbours and the notice of his death in *The Times* and the local paper contributed to a reasonable turnout to honour his burial. Many among the gathering she recognised. Some she had known since childhood, others she had met in the local pub when she popped in for a drink with her granddad. It was there they would hold the wake when they had said farewell.

The mud-spattered coffin in its last resting place, Sarah turned her back on the grave. Mourners approached to offer condolences. Deflecting her own tears, she thanked people for coming and made sure they knew where the wake was to be held. An elderly man she did not recognise held back from the others who moved towards their cars to escape the downpour. His slight stoop could not disguise what must once have been an impressive stature, now supported with a stick, and on his black suit he wore a row of medals.

'I hope you don't mind me attending. I saw the notice of death in the newspaper and felt I had to come. Douglas Harper. I'm sorry we meet at last under such circumstances.'

'Sarah Piper, John's granddaughter. Thank you for coming, have you come far?'

'From Cornwall, I came up to London on the train yesterday and stayed in a hotel overnight before coming here this morning,' answered Douglas.

Sarah scanned her memory for anything that might help place this gently-spoken man, but drew a blank.

'You're coming to the wake?' Sarah asked. 'Do you know where to go?'

'It's kind of you to offer – yes I'd like that, and no, I don't.'

While they had been talking the last of the mourners' cars drew out of the iron gates of the cemetery, leaving only the black Jaguar awaiting Sarah.

'Can I give you a lift?' she indicated towards the car.

'That's kind, I can ask in the pub if they can phone for a taxi to take me to the station later,' said Douglas.

Settled in the back, the man was first to break what could have been an uncomfortable silence.

'I suspect you are wondering who I am? That's a bit unfair really because it puts me at an advantage as I know a lot about you.'

'You do?' Vulnerable as she was, Sarah felt no threat from this courteous man but she was intrigued and slightly disconcerted that she had no inkling as to who he was. She had known her grandfather all her life and with her grandmother they had acted as her parents following the untimely death of both her mother and

7

father when she was just nine years old. But she had never heard mention of Douglas Harper.

'John was so proud of you,' said Douglas. 'We kept in touch with cards at Christmas and the occasional letter, although I hadn't seen him since the end of the war. Life took me abroad then and when I returned to England we never quite got round to meeting up, and now it's too late. I felt John was unsurprisingly reluctant to remember the war and blotted it out of his memory. He took the loss of his career much harder than the pain of losing his arm you know.'

Sarah didn't know. Her grandfather never spoke of the events that had caused his injury. All she knew was that he had been wounded in France around the time of the D-Day invasion of Europe. The normally open man, whom she had adored, would clam up if asked about that or any event that preceded it. She had learned very young not to upset him by asking about the past. What had Douglas meant about the loss of her grandfather's career?

'He was so pleased that you achieved what he could not,' Douglas continued. 'In a way I think you saved him. He could live his life through you.'

What did Douglas mean? The car was drawing up outside the pub and the conversation was left hanging. Sarah's thirst to learn more was eating her up, but her hosting duties kept her from continuing the chat with Douglas.

'It's lovely to meet you; we'll try and catch up later.'

The round of condolences and small talk did little to divert her from the pain of this extraordinary day and the curiosity that had been piqued by the elderly stranger.

Sitting alone eating a buffet lunch and sipping from a pint of bitter, Sarah tried to reach Douglas several times but on each occasion was hijacked by another well-meaning guest. As people began to trickle away she looked again for him but the seat where he had sat was empty. A shock ran through her that she might never find him again.

Turning round she glimpsed him at the bar. Relieved, and this time avoiding the departing guests, she crossed the room.

'I'm just ordering my taxi,' said Douglas as she approached. 'Thank you for the spread; it was a fine send off.'

'What you said about granddad, I would like to know more. I don't suppose you have time…' hesitated Sarah.

'Whilst I am still alive,' laughed Douglas, 'time is what I have plenty of.'

'How about now, if it's convenient? I'm going to granddad's house, there is so much to sort out and my car is there, it's only a short distance from here, we could take that taxi.'

'It would be a pleasure, it's not often I get a chance to reminisce. I can catch a train to London later and I'm not leaving for home until the morning,' he said with a smile.

As the cab drew up outside the cottage that had once been her home, Sarah felt an overwhelming sense of sadness. Everything this place had held for her now was reduced to memories and her emotions rose to the surface. Noticing a tear on her cheek, Douglas put a comforting arm around her and they walked together through the garden to the door.

Even in its recent state of neglect the garden was beautiful, the storm could not batter down the early flowering blooms and new spring growth bursting around her, the scent released by the rain hauntingly funereal.

'My grandparents loved this garden; granddad would spend hours weeding, watering or just sitting on his bench.' The grief Sarah had been holding back all day then hit her. At least before this morning she had had a life to look forward to, now that had gone too and sorrow consumed her. She collapsed on the wooden bench, where her grandfather had so often sat, and sobbed.

Unfazed, Douglas said nothing, just waiting for her tears to subside. Cried out, Sarah reached in her bag for the keys and passed them to the elderly man to open the door.

'A cup of tea, or maybe something stronger if I can find anything?' suggested Douglas, leading the distressed young woman to a sofa.

'Something stronger, I think. Usually some wine in the fridge, and whisky and gin on the sideboard in the dining room. I'm so sorry, I should be doing this,' Sarah said, half standing.

'Stay where you are. I can get it,' said Douglas leaving the room.

By the time he had returned with a bottle of wine and two small tumblers Sarah had pulled herself together.

'These glasses will do, won't they, they were the first I came to.'

'They're fine,' said Sarah as Douglas poured a tumbler each and took a seat on the armchair facing her.

The previous evening was the first time Sarah had returned to the house since she had learned of her granddad's death ten days earlier. A neighbour who came in to check on him had found John in bed. He had died in his sleep. Only the night before they had spoken on the phone as they did most evenings. John had been excited by his granddaughter's wedding plans, bursting with pleasure that she had asked him to walk her down the aisle. Now at least he would not suffer the disappointment of knowing that the wedding would not be happening.

As they nursed their glasses of wine, a silence settled which needed filling.

11

'Can I ask what you meant earlier when you mentioned granddad's pain at losing his career?' Sarah jumped in with the question that had been burning inside her.

'I don't know how much you know, maybe I have already said too much,' replied Douglas.

'Oh no, I want to find out. Granddad never said anything about his time during the war, or his life before it. As I got older I thought it was the trauma of losing his arm, so the subject was never broached.'

'I met your grandfather in Cairo when I was serving in North Africa. He was in Egypt recovering following his evacuation from Crete. He'd been hiding out in the mountains there since the fall of the island to the Germans in 1941. I was on leave from the front with the 7 th Armoured Division as we prepared for the final push at El Alemein in October 1942. I was a Desert Rat.

'Your granddad was little more than skin and bone when we first met, but we were drawn together through a mutual interest in music. I was nowhere near as good as him of course, but I dabbled a bit on the fiddle too.'

'He played the violin?' Sarah could not believe what she was hearing.

'Didn't you know? He wanted to become a professional musician, as you are, when the war ended. He hadn't a violin with

12

him in Cairo, but he did have this three-stringed instrument which he played on his knee with a bow.

'I had never encountered anything like it before, but the music he made was some of the most exhilarating and beautiful I had ever heard. He had that musician's knack of learning any instrument quickly. He could play the piano too and those skills made him much in demand.' Douglas noticed Sarah's continuing look of surprise.

'It's hard to believe, but despite a world on the edge of the apocalypse, Cairo was a party town. We had taken some heavy defeats in the desert and during those months, before the last battle of El Alamein, many were convinced Rommel's troops would make it all the way to Cairo.

'Away from the fighting, soldiers could let their hair down and briefly escape the horrors of war. We would party as if there was no tomorrow because, quite simply, there might not be one. There was more food and drink than the people could imagine back home in Britain, and many young women working as nurses, ambulance drivers and administrative support, liberated from the shackles of austerity felt free to join in the excitement.

'I can see this is all new to you, John never mentioned anything about it?'

'He always encouraged me to play music. He gave me my first violin when I was ten; I thought he had bought it second hand.

Sarah closed her eyes, and softly murmured 'It must have been his.' That she had not a clue about her granddad's past left her stunned.

'When you went off to study music and then got your first job with the orchestra, he wrote to me bursting with pride. Although we kept in contact over the years by post, we never met since our paths crossed again in 1944. It was pure coincidence. We had both been injured during the invasion of Europe.

His injuries were much worse than mine. I had taken a bullet through my hand from German troops fighting a rearguard action as we chased the retreating enemy inland from the French coast. Douglas had not been so fortunate; he was in an awful mess.

'What exactly happened he would not say, I suspected the nature of his work had been secret, maybe Special Services, but his left arm had been amputated and he was lucky to pull through from the infection which took hold as a result. When he came out of his fever, it was John who remembered me and later we were evacuated to England, to a stately home that had been requisitioned as a hospital somewhere in Surrey, to recuperate. By that time, he had reached the rank of major.

'Slowly he began to recover. We would talk most days but somehow he had changed, hardly surprising after the trauma he had endured. Now he remained guarded about what had happened and at first was reluctant to speak about his music.

'You see, we all had a light which we could hold on to, something that saw us through those dreadful times. For some it was a wife, children or a girlfriend, for him it had been music, and that light had been snuffed out. But, our shared love of music was what had brought us together. It was essential for him to engage with that part of his past if we were to communicate. Fortunately, if a bit reluctantly, he acquiesced.

'We lost touch soon after that. After my convalescence, they were keen to get me back to France. The Germans were being pursued across their home borders and, following their surrender in 1945, I was part of the occupying army on the Rhine.

'John was to have a much longer route to recovery but he found love in that hospital with one of the nurses who had tended him back to health. That was your grandmother.' Douglas smiled at Sarah.

'I didn't know that. They never spoke of how they met, just that it had been during the war. They were very happy together right up until granny's death ten years ago,' remembered Sarah.

'I always sensed they were happy, she put him back together, although that regret at not fulfilling his promise as a violinist was never far from the surface. We lost touch after that. It was not until some time after I was demobbed that I made contact again. By then I was married with a baby on the way.

'Through his regimental archives I discovered he had been awarded a Military Cross and it didn't take me long to trace his address from the newspaper cuttings and I contacted him by post.

'Your grandparents had moved to this house by that time. I had been right about John's Special Services background; his award had been for bravery behind enemy lines. That much was in the public domain, but he still resolutely refused to discuss it. He preferred to wipe it from his memory and by that time he was bound up with the family after the birth of your dad in 1950.

'Your grandparents could hardly have been happier and when you came along, to have a grandchild was just the icing on the cake. That of course was until their world was torn apart by the death of your dad and mum. But, like so many of our generation who had been witness to the horrors of war John was stoic in his grief and having you to look after probably helped save him.'

Sarah vividly remembered the day when her whole world had come crashing down. She had been woken to find the babysitter, a friend of her mum and dad's, there with her grandparents. Her granddad had broken the news about the car crash, a head on collision he said, they would have been killed instantly. She had run to him and he had hugged and hugged her so tight as if he could squeeze out the grief that overwhelmed her.

The recent loss of her granddad had been like losing her father and mother again. In one day, she felt she had lost everything. With her grandfather's death, she had been unable to go on the planned European concert tour with the orchestra and had resigned her contract. Her boss had been optimistic that a position would come up again, and her colleagues had been supportive, but for the time being she was jobless and could not even bury herself in work. Then the events of early that morning came back to her. How could that bastard have done it to her? Now she was all alone in the world.

Staring into the emptiness her sorrow gripped her by the throat and Sarah gulped for air as the tears again flooded down her face.

'I'm sorry; I didn't mean to upset you by bringing back memories of your mum and dad. It was insensitive of me,' Douglas crossed the room and sat beside her offering a shoulder to cry on.

'It's not what you said. I'm sorry, this is not fair on you and you've been so kind,' sobbed Sarah.

'Take your time, I'm not going anywhere, just let it all out,' soothed Douglas.

And Sarah did. In an unpunctuated torrent of sorrow, anger and despair the story of her fiancé's infidelity and how she had discovered it that very morning came pouring out. Everyone she had ever loved had now left her.

The night before the funeral she had stayed at her grandfather's house. Her fiancé, Gareth, was abroad on business and had arranged to come to the cottage direct from the airport that morning. Sarah had wanted to spend one last night in what she considered her childhood home. Petrified of how she would hold up reading the eulogy at the funeral service she stayed up well into the small hours, rewriting it over and over again. After a short, fitful sleep, she awoke with the sudden realisation that there was no printer in her grandfather's house. As it was early, she decided to drive the five miles home to the flat she had moved into with Gareth little over a year before, and print the document there.

At six o'clock in the morning, the traffic was light and she was there in no time. She let herself into the flat, opened her laptop and clicked to print the document on the wireless printer that sat in the corner on a table in the minimalist lounge diner. The printer clunked and whirred into action, then started churning out the eulogy she had worked so hard on that night.

'What's that?' she heard a sleepy woman from behind her bedroom door that adjoined the lounge.

Then the unmistakable voice of Gareth. 'What?'

'That noise,' said the woman.

'I can't hear anything, go back to sleep. Unless, now you're awake…?'

Sarah didn't wait to hear any more. Surely there must be an explanation? For only a second Sarah held on to that delusion before reality hit home. Calmly she walked to the printer, took her papers and crossed to the front door, silently letting herself out. She paused for a moment outside before walking away.

As she drove off, recognition of what she had just learned dawned on her and the tears began to fall. How long had this affair been going on? She went over in her mind the opportunities Gareth would have had to be unfaithful. She worked away a lot and was out most evenings playing with the orchestra. As a record company executive, he too travelled for his work. Before now she had never given a thought to the possibility of infidelity: they were in love, going to be married in a couple of months, have children, grow old together. How could he do this to her on the very day she was to bury the other man she loved most in the world?

In the end it didn't matter if it was an ongoing relationship or a one-night stand. That he was sleeping with another woman on the night before her granddad's burial was enough. It just went to prove what a callous, untrustworthy bastard he was. How had she not seen it coming? Why had there been no signs?

She drove on autopilot, thoughts playing on a loop in her head. The upset and anger fought for space with the cool realisation that she had had a lucky escape. That's what she had to keep telling herself to get her through the day and beyond. But, if she understood her good fortune in finding out about Gareth's philandering ways, why did she feel so wretched? Back outside the house, she reached for her phone and typed in the curt message, 'It's over. Hope she was worth it. I never want to see you again.'

The burial of her grandfather put into blunt contrast the two men in her life. One had nurtured, loved and provided for her since she had been a child; the other had lied, used and betrayed her. How could she have been so blind when she had the example of her granddad with whom to hold every other man up for comparison?

That he was of such greater worth, Sarah told herself, should make her stronger on this day in particular. She owed it to her grandfather to be brave.

Now, spilling out her heart to a virtual stranger, Sarah realised her granddad had been even stronger than she had realised. He had not wallowed in self-pity after all that he had been through, but had lived for the day and the future and flung himself into giving her the best opportunities that life could offer.

She could not imagine the pain he had suffered in losing his own son so young, the trauma of his disability and being unable to pursue his vocation in music and the loss of his wife, the woman who had saved him. All the while, he had protected her from the events of his past and channelled his love into her wellbeing.

With him as the most significant person in her life, how could she have fallen for the superficial charms of a man who had betrayed her so cheaply?

Douglas sat and listened as Sarah poured out emotions that flitted between anger, self-blame and relief at what she had escaped. Then the reality of her situation would strike and the tears would flow again.

Outside night was drawing in, and Douglas rose to draw the curtains. 'I don't like to leave you like this, but I should get back to London. Will you be OK?'

'You're welcome to stay,' Sarah said without hesitation. She found comfort in talking to this kind man who somehow allowed her to hold on to a connection with her grandfather, however fragile that link might be. 'I can make up a bed in one of the spare rooms.'

'Well,' said Douglas, 'that's very kind of you. I'd be happy to. I can get an early train to London tomorrow in time to pick up my bag from the hotel and get to Paddington to catch my train home. My grandson is meeting me at Truro in the afternoon.'

Sarah felt a wave of relief. All of a sudden, she realised that she did not want to be alone.

Late into the evening they talked, Sarah seeking solace in this gentle man who soothed her pain by listening, and fed her appetite to know about her granddad's past with stories of their encounters during the war. She asked him to start again from the beginning and tell her all the details.

Douglas recalled how he had first met John in Cairo. Following his debrief, John had been billeted in a house of some friends of Douglas's who told him the fellow officer had been evacuated by launch off the enemy-occupied island of Crete in the eastern Mediterranean.

'We met up at the house before going on to party. I was carrying my violin. A few of us had formed an impromptu band and we were, surprisingly, much in demand at get-togethers in the city, particularly after people had had a few drinks.

'He had been reserved, talking about his experiences on Crete but at the sight of the violin his eyes lit up and he became more animated.

'He asked me if he could have a go,' recalled Douglas, 'and immediately it was clear to all gathered there that he was a gifted musician. We invited him to play with the band that night but he said he could not take my place as we only had one violin.

'Then he disappeared to his room and came back carrying a battered music case. He struggled a bit with one of the catches before opening the case and almost reverentially lifting out an instrument I had never seen before. He called it a lyra and asked if we wouldn't mind if he played that. To him the instrument was something of a talisman as the case had deflected a bullet that might otherwise have killed him.

'There and then, he played us a song. I was transfixed. It was as though as he played he became one with the mystical instrument. That he should join us in the band that night was unquestionable.

'At first he started to join in with whatever we were playing, improvising. But as we heard the sound emanating from this strange instrument, our playing fell away.

'As John warmed to his performance, the only sound was that of the beautiful lyra rising and falling, casting a spell over the revellers there.

'Through our mutual love of music we clicked, and even in that short time we became firm friends. As with many wartime encounters, it was temporary, I was to return to my regiment in preparation for the coming counter offensive against Rommel's Afrika Korps and I heard that John had later gone east to the Canal Zone for specialist training.'

As they talked into the night Sarah found comfort in listening to stories about her grandfather and felt less alone in the world. Sometime in the early hours she nodded off, only to be woken by Douglas who suggested she go to bed. She would need all her strength for the coming days when she would have to sort out John's affairs.

Chapter 2

A SMALL OUTCROP of rock shielded by a curtain of scrub afforded John Piper some temporary respite from the attentions of the scorching sun and the screeching Stuka dive-bombers overhead. At any other time, his current place on earth might have been described as heavenly, but as he looked back on the craggy slope he had dragged his exhausted, hungry body up, he knew he was in a living hell.

Down the mountainside in the tiny coastal village of Chora Sfakion, in its streets and on the surrounding beaches, thousands of abandoned British, Australian and New Zealand troops awaited capture. The message had come through that there were to be no more ships. The evacuation had ended; it was every man for himself.

In the chaos John had been separated from his decimated unit and knew he had to make a choice, and fast. Sit tight and be captured by the German troops who had hounded them the forty miles or so across Crete's White Mountains, or take his chances hiding out alone in that same hostile environment.

His gaze could not escape the vast expanse of cobalt sea stretching south all the way to the safety of Egypt four hundred miles away. John hoped he had put enough distance between himself and the village. The Germans were unlikely to approach the surrendering Allied troops from the forbidding terrain in the west. More likely they would drop down through the Imbros Gorge, following the same path he had so recently taken trying to buy time for his retreating comrades. The troops had named this punishing route the 'Via Dolorosa' after the Way of Sorrow Christ had walked on his way to Calvary.

John weighed up the option of pushing on in the glaring heat of the day exposed to the scrutiny of enemy planes. Never having felt so weak, he decided to stay put, concealed on the mountain, before moving on under cover of darkness.

Trying not to succumb to the exhaustion he felt, the young army captain pondered on what had brought him to his present predicament. Alone on a Cretan mountainside, he thought back to happier times when his greatest hope was to become a musician.

The only child of a farm worker and his wife, John had lived much of his young life outdoors in the fields, helping with the harvests, hefting bales of hay and feeding the stock. He adored the freedom of the outdoors and would spend hours alone exploring the countryside around the farm. Although he was much loved, his parents had little time to indulge him and John was content to live in a world of adventures of his own making. He had grown up strong, sturdy and fit and it was a great surprise to his parents when he displayed a love and gift for music after picking up a school friend's violin. Nobody was sure where his ability came from, but his parents were keen to nurture their son's prodigious talent.

He was the first person in his family accepted to college. His parents had been amazed but proud when his hours of practising had led to his winning a scholarship.

With the outbreak of war and conscription impending, John volunteered. As an undergraduate he was earmarked for officer training and sent to Sandhurst from where, upon passing out, he took a commission in the Royal Artillery. Despite his artistic sensibilities, his strength, love of adventure and physical stature made him a natural soldier and hearing of the formation of a new commando group he asked to be considered. To his surprise, he was accepted and in early 1941 the unit was sent to Egypt before being deployed in Crete.

By the time the commandos landed in Souda Bay on the north of Crete on the night of 26th May, the battle was all but lost. Originally destined to attack German lines of communications and turn the tide in the conflict, the unit was instead commanded to cover the retreating army as it made its way south across the mountains in the hope of being evacuated by the Royal Navy. The operation had been a partial success and 6,000 troops had got off the beaches. But under increased air attack with the Germans closing in it was abandoned and 5,000 troops were left behind.

John's natural instincts as a commando were to fall back on his training and hide out in the mountains, preferring to risk death than become a prisoner of war. As the sun dropped down behind the towering peaks to the west the air cooled and he determined to strike out and put more distance between himself and the advancing enemy. The Stukas would not fly in the dark and if his calculation was correct that the Germans would be concentrating their forces on the surrendered Allied troops on the beaches, he could buy himself time.

Easing himself out of his hideaway he stretched his aching body before setting off, slowly picking his way upwards in the moonlight.

'*Kalispera*. Good evening English.'

A disembodied voice, clear yet quiet, cut through the night air like a slingshot. Training told John to hit the ground; he reached for his revolver and looked around for cover.

The only suitable refuge was a huge boulder fifteen yards away but as his eyes adjusted in the darkness he could see he was already too late. Sitting on top of the rock, silhouetted by the moon behind him sat the owner of the voice.

'Don't shoot, you'll alert the Germans.' The man laughed climbing down from his perch. In one hand he carried a herdsman's crook and with the other he tucked a handgun into his belt alongside a menacing looking knife. In the moonlight it was difficult to tell his age, but he moved across the hillside towards John with the sprightliness of youth and the confidence of someone who had strode these mountains for a lifetime.

'My English is not so good, but better than your Greek maybe?' The bearded man was about his own age. As he got closer John could see he was dressed all in black with trousers tucked in to knee-length boots and he wore a kind of tasselled scarf around his head.

The stranger held out a hand. John slowly rose, loosening the grip on his firearm.

'Andreas,' the young man introduced himself.

'John,' he said and took Andreas' hand.

'You did well, I have been watching you climb, you are a mountain goat. You must be thirsty and hungry. Drink now and eat, we are fine for the moment but soon we must move.'

Andreas reached into a bag and motioned John to sit. Pulling out some bread, he ripped off a large chunk and handed it to the soldier before reaching in again for some hard cheese that he roughly cut with his knife. Opening his water bottle he proffered it to John who drank thirstily before realising it might be the only water the Greek man had. Understanding his reticence, Andreas waved him on. 'Drink, there is plenty of water just down there.'

John stared out into the abyss, but all he could see were the mountains dropping off steeply into the black infinity of the Libyan Sea.

'I will take you somewhere safe; the Resistance will look after you. But first we must walk a bit. The Germans are too busy now taking prisoners on the beach but soon they will try to conquer the mountains. That I think they will find not so easy. Have this for the journey.' Andreas put a hand into the pocket of his baggy black trousers and pulled out a flask, unscrewed the top and took a swig.

'*Yamas, eleftheria*! Cheers, to freedom!' He passed the bottle to John who followed suit.

The liquid burned as John spluttered and Andreas laughed.

'Raki, made in my village. Now we can do anything.'

'Thank you,' John said but was not so sure he meant it.

'*Efharisto*,' instructed Andreas. 'That is thank you in Greek. *Parakalo*, You're welcome. *Parme*, let's go.'

Whether it was the fiery spirit or the water and food he didn't know, but John felt revitalised. Meeting this man of the mountains had lifted his mood. The young herdsman slung the pack over his shoulder, picked up his crook and set off up the slope. His course was sure-footed and silent and John marvelled at how at one his guide seemed with this treacherous terrain.

Climbing to the top of the mountain they took time to stand and survey all around them. To the north and west as far as the eye could see the mountains rose and rose like angry waves cresting on a sea of sky.

'Behind us is Mount Kastro, the fortress, to the left is Pachnes the tallest in the White Mountains, and to the west the Gorge of Samaria. But we must go down.' To John's surprise, Andreas set off downhill in the direction of the coast. 'I told you, *nero*, water. There is plenty there.'

The two men progressed down the mountainside, the leader adroitly navigating boulders, bushes and clumps of oleander shrubs, whilst John tried to follow in his footsteps, and keep up a good pace without turning an ankle.

After they had descended what seemed like many hundreds of feet, the going got easier as they hit a track. Here the two men could walk side by side in a silent amity built solely on trust. John could hear the gentle rippling of the sea caressing the pebbles on the shoreline somewhere below.

The path led down onto a shingle beach nestling beneath the cliffs they had just navigated. A row of stunted trees grew through the pebbles, casting shadows in the moonlight.

'Glyca Nera, Sweet Waters we call this bay,' Andreas said at last. Puzzled, John watched as he took his water bottle and dropped to his knees, digging through the pebbles. Within minutes he dipped his bottle into the hole and filled it with water.

'Here, taste.' He offered John the bottle.

Tentatively he took a sip, before gulping down mouthfuls of cold, fresh water.

'The water is a gift from the mountains. It flows though the hills and comes up here,' explained Andreas.

John listened as Andreas told him how the water filtered down from the mountain peaks through cracks in the rocks to emerge as springs on the beach. It truly was a welcome gift from these austere mountains.

Eager to wash away the stench of battle, stripping down, John waded into the sea, the underwater flows of freezing water mingling with the warm salty Aegean.

'We must go, *ella*, come. We have to find shelter before dawn,' Andreas urged.

From the far end of the beach the track re-emerged, clinging to the side of the cliff. A lone white chapel stood out in the darkness, casting a moon shadow across an otherwise desolate landscape.

Time passed slowly. There was a comforting reassurance in the stillness of the wild mountains. John felt so small in the vastness of the terrain, which momentarily gave him a sense that he could never be found, an idea he knew to be untrue.

Stopping, Andreas pointed along the path that dropped down the mountainside ahead. 'There is Loutro, where we will stay today.'

As the early summer dawn began to break they descended into a huddle of small white cottages beside a crescent bay guarded out to sea by the dark shadow of an island. A few fishing caiques were drawn up on the narrow beach. The two men silently skirted the seafront before slipping down a narrow cobbled path between two houses. Without knocking a door was opened and they were ushered inside.

The single room was lit by a flickering oil lamp revealing three men, dressed like Andreas, all in black. The oldest of the men spoke first.

'*Kalimera* Andreas.' Turning to John, 'Welcome to Loutro. Good morning English, I am Spyros. *Katse kato*, sit down.' Spyros motioned towards a table and as he sat, another of the men, unbidden, placed upon it glasses and a carafe of clear liquid.

32

It was apparent to John that the man who addressed him was the leader. His hair was still black but his greying moustache and hint of a belly suggested a long life well lived and the andarte's commanding voice felt at home in his muscular, rugged body.

The five men sat and Spyros poured the raki. 'Today is a sad day, but we must drink to freedom. *Eleftheria*!'

The passionate toast raised by Spyros was matched by the fiery spirit John had first experienced earlier that night on the mountainside.

'We must sleep now. Tonight you will accompany me to my goddaughter's wedding.' Seeing John's surprise Spyros reassured the English soldier. 'You are safe here for the moment, the only way to Loutro is by boat or across the mountains. There is no road for the Nazi motorbikes and lookouts are posted on all the tracks.'

Despite his precarious predicament, exhaustion from the hike across the mountains and the raki soon saw him asleep on a rough bed that had been made for him on the mezzanine. The next he knew, he was being shaken awake in the dim light.

'Wake up English. Captain John we must get ready to move soon.' Spyros was kneeling beside the bed. 'First eat.'

Through the half-opened shutters John could see that dusk was already falling. He remembered what Spyros had said about the wedding. He had not been joking. He hungrily tucked into the bread, cheese and mountain greens that had been laid out for him on the table before being told to change into the bundle of clothes Spyros handed him.

'Wear these,' commanded Spyros. 'We will make you a Greek shepherd,' he laughed. 'We will burn your uniform. You are less likely to be caught dressed like this, but if you are,' smiling he drew his hand across his throat, 'you will be executed by the Germans as a spy.'

'I'll take my chances,' said John, already stripping off his uniform.

'I hope it will not come to that. Here, hurry now. We have a wedding to go to and our boat leaves in half an hour. As soon as night falls.'

Leaving the cottage as the light faded John could still make out the splendour of the place he found himself. The half moon bay was dotted with whitewashed cottages facing seawards beneath the seemingly impenetrable mountains. Beside a jetty fashioned of boulders a caique some ten metres in length was moored, a crewman tending the lines and the captain ready at the wheel.

'*Kalo taxidi*, have a good journey. I must leave you here,' said Andreas as Spyros and the two other men ushered John aboard.

'Thank you, Andreas,' John was sad to leave the man who had aided his escape.

'*Efharisto*, you are Greek now,' smiled the young Cretan as he turned and walked from the quay.

Aboard the caique the lines were quickly cast off and the boat headed away from shore setting a course further west, hugging the shadows of the sheer cliffs which cascaded into the sea. There were no other vessels on the horizon. The only sound to be heard was the low thud of the engine over the whisper of the wake as it met the rocky shore. It was hard to imagine that the world was at war. From where John was at that moment, peace seemed infinite.

Below deck, the men talked. Spyros confirmed John's fears that the island had now fallen to the Germans and that similar evacuations to the one at Chora Sfakion had been attempted from Heraklion. At the surrender, 12,000 troops were stranded on the island waiting to be taken prisoner.

'If the Germans think they can ever truly conquer our people, they are in for a big surprise,' Spyros thumped his fist hard on the galley table. 'Raki, let's drink. We are going to a wedding.'

A flask was uncorked and the crewman joined them in the toast 'E*leftheria y thanatos*', freedom or death. Spyros pointed to the blue and white naval ensign of Greece streaming from a staff at the stern of the boat. He explained how it expressed exactly that, the nine syllables of that Greek call to arms represented by the nine stripes on the flag.

'We will never accept the rule of any foreign power. However long it takes, we will be free again.'

They spoke of how already the Resistance movement was taking shape and that some British intelligence officers had made headway in encouraging unity between Greek clan chiefs even before the invasion. Cretan messengers were already passing information across the island and in the following days they would have a clearer picture of the state of the island under occupation.

They were called on deck as the captain edged the bow of the caique towards a shelving shingle shore. Leaping into the water, the crewman walked the bowline to the beach, securing it to a rock.

'From here we travel alone,' said Spyros, handing John a carved, wooden crook. 'You are now a shepherd.'

Spyros jumped into the shallow water and helped John down from the prow of the vessel. With his charges safely ashore, the crewman climbed back aboard.

'*Adio*,' the men said their goodbyes as the skipper put his craft astern and set sail east for Loutro.

The two men picked their way across a pebble beach, following upstream the valley of a small river which cut a path from the White Mountains to the sea. Ahead the mountains through which it had carved its course.

'This is the great gorge of Samaria, the longest in Europe. The wedding is to be held in the middle of the canyon where we will not get any unwelcome guests,' Spyros explained. 'Follow me and look at the ground as we walk and you will be fine.'

The pebbles gave way to boulders and rocks as they began to climb, crossing the river back and forth on impromptu bridges made of tree trunks, the going getting tougher as the sides of the gorge closed in on them.

Soon the moon was invisible. Without looking directly upwards it was impossible to see the brilliant stars which dotted the night sky. At one point John reckoned the walls of the canyon were just ten feet apart and towered above for more than one thousand feet.

'These are the "gates". To us, they open to our sanctuary. To the Germans they will lead to hell.' Spyros raised a hand and signalled for John to stop behind him. A single whistle broke the silence.

'*Yasoo*, Manoli,' Spyros spoke into the darkness.

Looking up, the shadow of a man clutching a rifle could be seen perched on a rock just above their heads.

'Welcome Spyro and friend, how are things,' greeted Manolis.

'All is good,' replied Spyros, turning to John and laughing. 'Manolis could hold back the whole German army from here, alone. If they ever were to get off the beach!'

Having fought his way across the island, trying to hold back the relentless tide of a ruthless enemy willing to sustain any losses to subdue their foe, John was unconvinced by Spyros' ebullient confidence in the impregnability of the gorge. A part of his mind was unable to shake the anxiety of his precarious predicament.

Spyros threw the man his flask. Manolis took a good measure of raki. '*Stin ygeia sas*, cheers, *sto kalo*, go with the good.'

They bade him farewell, *adio*, and the two men struck out further into the gorge.

As they climbed in silence, the isolation was manifest. John felt the security this place afforded more than made up for any jeopardy in the climb through the darkness.

Eventually the canyon opened, breaking into a clearing.

'This is the church of Osia Maria,' announced Spyros.

John struggled to see anything in the dark but as they continued forward he made out the outline of a chapel with an arched roof.

'This church has been here since Byzantine times and is named after Saint Maria of Egypt. It is from this that the gorge takes its name Samaria. The canyon has never been conquered. Even when the whole of Greece was overrun by the Ottomans, they couldn't secure the great gorge.' Proudly Spyros led the way to the other side of the glade and through a thicket of plane trees.

It had been some hours since they had left Loutro, and already high above them, John made out the new dawn. He could smell the heady scent of wild camomile, sage and oregano, and hear the tinkling of goat bells as the new day battled to take hold in the canyon.

A few cottages emerged by the side of the river and John thought it must be the most remote village he had ever encountered. The bells along with piles of wood, some beehives and a grove of olive trees were the only clues as to how people might survive in this cut off place.

Spyros made his way to the cottages and opened a door. In the front room of a house, it seemed a small taverna had been set up. After their long climb, John was grateful to take the weight off his feet and they sat at an empty table. Several men were drinking coffee and water and within minutes the same drinks were put down in front of the two travellers. John quickly lost what was being said as they were surrounded by well-wishers. A welcome meal of boiled eggs, cheese, yoghurt, honey and bread was placed on the table, and as the two men ate hungrily, Spyros held animated conversation with the villagers.

Turning to John, Spyros explained, 'My goddaughter and the groom are from Paleochora to the west. In different times they would wed there but now it is safer for them to marry here. They arrived yesterday by boat and the ceremony is at noon in the church of Agios Nikolaos further up the canyon.'

Accompanied by a group of guests, Spyros and John made their way steadily up the gorge. The conversation was all of local matters, families, friends and livestock – the war that raged the other side of these protective mountains banished from their thoughts. Nothing was allowed to spoil the big day.

There were many more guests outside than within the walls of the tiny church. The groom was waiting nervously at the church door as the bride arrived with her entourage. Spyros elbowed his way inside saying, 'I will be back later,' leaving John outside amongst a crowd of men. The air was thick with the smoke of a hundred strong cigarettes. Nobody seemed surprised at his presence and many approached, hugging him or slapping him on the back.

Once the ceremony was over, Spyros emerged and grabbed John to stand next to him as the newly married couple emerged, passing through a long line offering greetings of '*Na zisete*, long life to you' accompanied by gifts of money, these last piled on a plate carried by a groomsman.

The wedding party wound its way slowly back down the gorge, singing to the accompaniment of a musician playing an instrument Spyros told John was a laouto, similar to a lute. While they were gone, the open space at the centre of the village had been transformed. Tables were laid, everywhere flags fluttered from impromptu staffs and a lamb and goat turned on spits above a fire pit. In the warm of the afternoon sun, the men welcomed the opportunity to discard their jackets over the backs of chairs.

A group of musicians sat on stools set aside for them tuning instruments, as women of the village placed jugs of wine on the tables. Spyros sat John next to him near the bride and groom. Plates laden with food were brought to the tables, toasts were shouted as the cacophony increased to fever pitch. Even if John had been able to understand what was going on around him, he would have struggled to disentangle one conversation from another. Gunshots were fired into the air as the bride and groom danced with their families and friends.

At first John was drawn by the familiar melody of a fiddle being played, joining the laouto, a guitar and some bagpipes. But there was another extraordinary sound which dominated the music, the like of which he had never heard before. Through the crowd, John looked to see from where this imposing, heroic melody was emanating. At the centre of the band, he made out the lead musician bowing an instrument that resembled a three-stringed violin but played with a bow, upright on the musician's knee.

Immediately the music made an emotional connection and the other instruments sank into the background. It was not his trained musical sensibilities that drew him in, but something more fundamental. He had never experienced a sound so firmly rooted in the landscape, as though it had sprung fresh from the soil and was talking to the earth that had just given birth to it. At once John was entranced. He knew, even at that time of jeopardy, that he was

41

experiencing something that would change his life. In that instant he could not imagine the music being played anywhere else or at any other moment. He felt he was hearing an instrument that he had been waiting all his life to hear, if only he had known it. The sound articulated feelings so primal that it rose above the worldly space. Staring up to the heavens, John saw the sun was dropping down behind the steep rock face. High above, from its mountain eyrie, a golden eagle took flight, silhouetted across the setting sun.

Spyros leant across and shouted above the music at John, his mouth full of roast goat. 'The lyra player, the leader of the group, he will be your guide. You will stay with him after the wedding until you are rescued. I will introduce you later, Vassilis speaks some English.'

As quickly as plates of food were emptied they were cleared away and replaced. Lamb roasted with rosemary, sage, wild garlic, lemon juice and olive oil and salted goat turned over the fire and seasoned with oregano kept arriving at the table. Hungry though he had been after his ordeal, John struggled to match the prodigious appetites of his hosts.

'Captain, may I sit?' The lyra player drew up a chair between Spyros and the English soldier.

Vassilis was a young man, no older than John, but his presence appeared more than his average build would suggest and, although dressed in the familiar attire of the men of the mountains, somehow he stood out from the crowd. His eyes sparkled, his smile easy and every move he made seemed in tune with his place on earth. Even without his lyra the musician carried with him some of the mysterious vigour which had resonated through his playing. John immediately felt that they would be friends and soon they fell into animated conversation firmly rooted in their mutual love of music.

If John's love of playing the violin was the passion in his life, he could sense that for the young Cretan music was more than that, it was life itself. When he talked of the lyra, his eyes revealed that it was fundamental to his existence, the very essence of his being.

When the musicians resumed playing it was not long before Vassilis called for the Englishman to join his group and the Cretan fiddle player willingly relinquished his instrument so their guest could perform. At first the new band member was tentative, improvising as he felt his way into the heart of the music. To start with his classical technique struggled to keep pace with the demonic speed and fire of Vassilis' performance but, shedding the conventions of his musical legacy, he gave himself to the tune and let it take him where it would.

Playing on, he became more comfortable with the rhythms and shapes woven by the lyra he was accompanying. Maybe it was the raki but in no time he felt as confident as if he had been playing these songs for a lifetime and when Vassilis called on him to perform a solo John felt assured enough to take centre stage and render a traditional Irish folk melody from his repertoire.

The immediate bond John had felt with Vassilis was now sealed. Handing back the violin, John resumed his seat. With hunger now satisfied by the feast, a young man took the floor in front of the musicians. Another, then several more joined him, arms around each other's shoulders slowly stepping left and right flicking out their feet in unison.

Leading on the lyra, Vassilis began to wind up the tempo and, as he did the dancers kept pace. The man who had first taken the floor led the dance from the start of the line, holding up a red scarf, acrobatically leaping into the air and slapping the heel of his boot with his free hand.

As the music took wing, the dancer's jumps got higher, always at one with the rhythm. The crowd clapped and shouted encouragement. Faster and faster Vassilis drew his bow across the strings until it seemed impossible the dancer could keep up but he never dropped a step, drawn along by the power of the lyra. Glistening with sweat he never fell behind the rhythm, his jumps becoming more spectacular until the music reached its crescendo; and stopped.

As the dancers left the floor to applause, a group of women led by the bride – in the traditional long white pinafore dresses or red skirts trimmed in gold covered with embroidered white aprons –

took their place for a similar, if less acrobatic dance. Endless carafes of wine and *carafakia* of raki kept arriving at the tables, conversation snatched in shouts, smiles and mime.

Spyros would not take no for an answer as he dragged John to his feet. If the young commando had been comfortable performing the music, the thought of dancing to it played on all of his natural inhibitions. Sandwiched between Spyros and another guest, his reticence quickly vanished as he followed their lead and let the music take him. Cries of '*Opa*' and '*Bravo*' bolstered his confidence as the pace quickened and he was pulled relentlessly towards the climax of the dance.

Invigorated yet exhausted, John collapsed onto his seat but it was not long before he was cajoled to retake the floor to dance and then by the musicians to play with them again. And so the night went on...

A hand gently shaking his shoulder awoke John from the soundest of sleeps. Blinking hard, it took him some moments to adjust to his whereabouts.

'*Kalimera*, good morning John, we should be moving on soon.' Vassilis stood over him as the commando felt his way into consciousness. The musician then busied himself by the fire in the small cottage, filling a long-handled *kafebriko* with coffee, sugar and water before bringing the coffee pot to a simmer over the flames. Pouring the coffee into a small cup he passed it to John then filled a glass from a water carrier that stood in the corner of the room and handed that to the soldier.

When he stepped out into the early morning, there was little sign of the wedding feast of the previous night save for the still smoking embers of the fire. Looking upwards he saw daylight but there was no sign of the sun from which it emanated above the towering cliffs. A mist arose from the scrubland and hovered between the ground and the canopy of plane, pine and cypress trees. Vassilis handed a pack to John and slung a black instrument case across his shoulders and picking up their crooks they headed out of the village into the mountains.

Chapter 3

THE HESITANT LIGHT of dawn seeped around the dark drapes on the windows and reached into the corners of the room. The rain had gone, leaving the watery sunlight to wash the early morning with the promise of a new day. Despite the late night, Sarah felt stirrings of optimism that would have seemed impossible the night before.

Popping to the corner store for eggs, bread and bacon, she rustled up breakfast before driving Douglas to the station. She watched as he walked into the ticket office; this calm, comforting man to whom she already owed so much for restoring some equanimity to her life. She felt better knowing that he was there for her. They had exchanged contact details and Sarah knew Douglas had meant it when he said she could get in touch at any time.

Sitting with a coffee she listed things she needed to do. Her grandfather, it seemed, had his affairs well in order. A row of neatly labelled box files sat on a shelf in his study. She reached for the file marked 'Will etc', lifted it down and opened the box.

The document had been updated just a month after her grandmother had passed away a decade ago and clipped to the top was a handwritten note.

Sarah

It appears I am dead. Do not mourn me long, this comes to us all and I have had a better life than most. That I have had that is in no small measure down to the love you have shown and the joy you have given me.

Quite simply, when your father and mother died, having you to look after saved our lives and when your grandmother passed you became the centre of my universe.

To do something you love with your life is a precious gift, and you already have that. Go on and conquer the world.

Love you always,

Granddad

A tear fell, smudging the blue ink of the handwritten letter. That her grandfather had so rarely expressed emotion made the note all the more poignant, and Sarah took comfort from the words.

Unclipping the note, she read the document beneath. Through the legal jargon it looked as though she was her grandfather's sole beneficiary. She dialled the number of Morton & Spicer, the solicitors who had drawn up the will, and arranged an appointment the next day to discuss the estate.

The job of collating his affairs was not as daunting as she had first feared. Each file was clearly labelled and on top of the contents was an up-to-date summary of the current assets. Pulling together documents relating to his bank and building society accounts and other investments, she listed anyone she thought might need to be told of the death for the solicitor. The most pressing of these had already been informed at the time she had registered the death the day after his passing.

It would be distressing clearing out the house, but that could wait for another day when the exact status of the estate had been confirmed. She walked through the cottage, feeling strangely at a loss as to what she should do. Tidy and uncluttered; her granddad's home had never had that dated feel of the houses of some elderly people.

As evening fell, Sarah began to feel the sense of her loss more acutely. Alone in the house she had lived in with her granddad for so many years she now struggled to hold on to that connection. Sarah felt a moment of panic at the thought of losing the special bond they had always shared.

Climbing the stairs, she noticed the hatch that went into the loft. As a young girl she had been up there, but had been warned off exploring by her grandfather, afraid she might fall through the floor. A pole with a hook on the end stood in the corner of the airing cupboard in the bathroom and she had seen her granddad use it to release the ladder to the attic. Tentatively she pushed on the hatch and it sprung open. She gently lowered the steps to the ground.

Slowly ascending, Sarah felt like a child exploring a secret domain. Sticking her head through the hatch, she found a switch screwed to the eaves. The light revealed a large space with some loft boards laid on the floor joists. The tidiness echoed the neat efficiency of the box files she had just examined. There was an oil-filled radiator, a fold-away canvas camp bed in a wooden casing, a box of old 78 rpm records and tucked in the far corner a green metal chest, its lid secured with a hasp and staple but no padlock. It was easy to slip the catch.

The smell of mothballs hit her. The contents of the trunk were covered by an army great coat. It was protectively draped over what appeared to be a dress uniform in a suit carrier, a biscuit tin which revealed a wealth of campaign medals, and a padded box which Sarah snapped open to reveal a medal, a silver cross on a ribbon of purple and white. This must be her grandfather's Military Cross that Douglas had told her about, modestly hidden away for all these years.

The coarse cloth of the old uniforms, the comfortable smell of the past and the sight of his possessions that had been hidden away for so long gave that moment an almost religious intensity Sarah could not fathom. Delving deeper into the trunk, nestled at the bottom, Sarah came across a black, hard case that immediately captivated her interest. Lifting it out she struggled to undo one of two rusted catches that was badly dented. Persevering, she managed to open the leather-covered case to reveal a dusty musical instrument and bow, protected in a cushion of dark blue silky material.

What had Douglas called it? This must be the Cretan lyra he had told her about. Sarah carefully lifted it from its case and ran her hands over the pear-shaped soundboard with its two semi-circular holes. She lightly plucked the three strings that ran up the carved fingerboard to the neck and peg box. As she dragged her finger across the dusty curved body the beauty of the grained wood was revealed. As a musician it tugged at something deep within her. She had to play it.

Gently putting the lyra back in its case, she carefully descended the steps, cradling it in her arms. Back in the living room, using a duster she wiped it clean. She would polish it later when she got her cleaning materials from the flat, along with her violins and other personal belongings.

Plucking the strings, she had no idea of what the tuning should be, but whatever it was, the lyra was not in tune. Despite this, Sarah sensed something magical about this strange instrument that her granddad had brought back from Crete. Slowly risking the fragile bow over the taut gut, she coaxed a noise from the lyra that, although dissonant in tone, promised a wealth of possibilities.

That night, somehow Sarah found comfort in the mysterious instrument, its discovery giving her an intangible link to her grandfather's past, much of which she had only discovered the day before from Douglas. In her heart she felt that her granddad had meant her to have the lyra and already, as she fell asleep, she knew it would be a talisman to help her through the difficult times which lay ahead.

The next morning she resorted to the internet to find out what she could about this unusual instrument. In no time she found the information, but was diverted by videos of artists playing lyra. Transfixed, by the time she returned to the task of tuning she was beguiled, not only by her emotional attachment to the music, but also the exciting prospect learning to play might hold for her.

Recognising the virtuosity of the performers, Sarah was aware of the years of practice that must have gone in to reach such heights. But as a musician she knew she had the knowledge, aptitude and determination to embark on that journey.

Surfing the net, it became clear there were many different types of lyra and tunings varied radically. She derived that hers was a common Cretan lyra, often tuned 'a d g'. She got the tuning app up on her smart phone and twisted the first peg. After what must be nearly 70 years of neglect the peg was resistant. Then it yielded. The gut string snapped.

'Damn'.

Searching for somewhere to buy lyra strings, she was surprised to find a site that not only sold strings but offered lessons. Her inquiry got an instant reply. A few emails later and Sarah had arranged to travel to north London in two days time to get the lyra restrung and have a lesson with a tutor who had introduced himself as Yannis.

Keen to explore the potential of the instrument, her plans had been thwarted by the broken string. Unable to see a solicitor until the next day, Sarah was forced to confront the issue she was desperately trying to avoid. She needed to move her possessions out of the flat. Perhaps it was cowardly but she didn't relish confrontation with Gareth. She didn't want feeble excuses, apologies or to rekindle the anger bumping into her ex fiancé would promote.

Gareth had not even had the balls to reply to her text. As far as Sarah was concerned, it was better that way. He would be at work now and she was not homeless, she could stay at the cottage until she had sorted out her granddad's affairs.

In the afternoon traffic the familiar journey took much longer than on the morning of the funeral, which now seemed a lifetime ago. Over and over Sarah buttressed her confidence by reminding herself how fortunate she was to be rid of Gareth. What had she ever seen in him? The love and pride her grandfather had expressed in his letter gave her strength.

With his counsel to 'go on and conquer the world' in her head, she packed clothes in suitcases, filled boxes with books, CDs and sheet music, loaded the boot and carefully placed her three precious violins on the back seat of the car. Closing the door to the flat she posted the key through the letterbox.

Pulling out of the parking spot, she felt a strange elation. She was going home, to the place where she had been brought up, to the security of that familiarity.

She hung clothes in the wardrobe of her childhood bedroom and stacked books in the study. Then she could hardly wait to take a bottle of polish and some dusters from a music case and set to work. With a slightly damp cloth she rubbed the arched back of the instrument, working from the bottom of the body along the back of the fingerboard to its neck and carved peg box. Gently she applied pressure with two fingers through the cloth, rubbing in a circular motion first one way then the other.

As she worked across the curved back of the lyra, an engraved eagle in flight emerged carved in the straight grained wood. Under the caress of her fingers the crafting of the beautiful instrument was slowly revealed. Sarah thought the body and fingerboard were made from walnut or a similar wood and remarkably the body, neck and peg box were carved from a single piece of timber.

Turning the instrument over, she began the same process on the soundboard. This was made of lighter wood, a beguiling, unblemished face contrasted with the ebony black of the fingerboard. She decided to remove the other two strings as they were likely to break and could be replaced when she visited her new-found teacher in London.

Three hours of painstaking work later, the lyra revealed its true glory. The natural beauty of the wood now shone through; it had survived the ravishes of time well. Looking at the result of her handiwork, Sarah felt a flush of excitement. She was reminded of how she felt as a little girl when she first opened the case revealing the violin given to her as a present by her granddad.

Her grandparents had done everything they could to make that Christmas a happy one. She now realised the emotional effort that must have taken them after the loss of their son and daughter-in-law, her mother and father, just nine months earlier.

For the ten-year-old Sarah the cottage was magical. A large Christmas tree twinkled with coloured lights and was laden with baubles, candy canes and golden foil-wrapped chocolate coins and nearly reached the low ceiling of the lounge where a fire roared in the grate and Christmas songs emanated from the tape deck.

She had been thoroughly spoiled. A set of Lego, a box of watercolours and a new bike she remembered, alongside the lucky coin, sweets and an orange. Family Christmases had always been spent at the cottage, so it was not difficult for her grandparents to reproduce the atmosphere of those happy times before the accident.

The excitement of waking on Christmas morning, emptying the stocking on her bed before breakfast and then opening presents around the tree before lunch had diverted Sarah's thoughts from her loss, although now she realised that easing the pain for her must have made that of her grandparents so much harder to bear.

It was only after lunch when her grandparents were in the kitchen washing up and Sarah was left alone with her presents that she felt melancholy wash over her. Time was beginning to heal the pain but always, somewhere was the dark cloud of grief waiting to blow across the sunniest of days. Her granddad was always sensitive to her thoughts, knowing instinctively when to head them off with a well-timed diversion or consoling her with a reassuring hug.

That Christmas, still wearing their crumpled paper hats, her grandparents snuggled up with Sarah between them on the sofa and leafed through a photo album of Christmases past. Granddad had hugged her as the tears fell. Even now Sarah remembered that strong man struggling to contain his emotions. Then he got up to get them Christmas cake, a cola for Sarah and tea for her grandmother and himself. Putting the tray on the low table he left the room, some time later returning with a large, brightly-wrapped present, and placed it in Sarah's arms.

'This is something we forgot to give you earlier,' granddad smiled. 'I hope it brings you great pleasure always.'

Although her grandfather was glowing, Sarah could feel a deference in his words which touched her deep inside. Tingling with excitement she stared at the unexpected gift.

'Go on, open it,' granddad urged, almost as excited as Sarah.

She needed no more encouragement, but with an attempt at some restraint slowly tore open the paper. A satisfying clunk as she flicked the catches was followed by almost unbearable anticipation before she lifted the lid.

On that Christmas Day, the desire had taken her by surprise. She didn't know where the passion had come from. Now she was aware of what she felt. It was that feeling Sarah felt when she had seen her first violin, that overwhelming desire to be able to play on seeing the lyra. She would have to be patient. Back then she had to contain herself until the New Year before she could begin lessons, surely as an adult she could wait two days?

Sarah had been a good student from the start; her violin teacher, Mrs Glynn, told her grandfather she had great natural ability, something Sarah now realised was probably inherited. But there was also a beauty in playing music which took her away from all the sorrow of her past and made life worth living.

By the time she started at comprehensive school she was considered good enough to join the senior orchestra, and soon was performing solos at concerts. She taught herself piano on the old upright in her grandfather's study and hearing her one day he realised she was proficient at that too. But it was the violin which was her first love and within three years the magnanimous Mrs Glynn advised John that if Sarah was to achieve her potential she would have to change to a new teacher.

Each week from then John would accompany his granddaughter on the train to London, insisting on carrying her violin case in his one arm leaving her with a briefcase bulging with sheet music and tapes. The lessons took her playing to new levels and by the age of fifteen she had achieved Grade 8 in her music exams and after an audition was accepted by the National Youth Orchestra.

By the time she entered the sixth form at school she was determined to follow a career as a professional musician and although she struggled to get a C grade in her history A-level, two top grades in Music and English Literature along with a strong audition saw her accepted into London's Royal College of Music as an undergraduate.

Remembering that delicious prospect of setting out on a musical adventure she had felt that Christmas, Sarah reached for her phone and feasted on YouTube videos of lyra music before downloading random albums from Nikos Xilouris, Ross Daly, Kostas Mountakis and Stelios Petrakis.

The names meant nothing to Sarah, but their music touched her, the melodies seeping inside her. She felt every draw of the bow on the strings as the music increased in intensity and pace, rising and falling until it reached its apogee. Already the lyra had weaved its magic and she was under its spell.

The following day she grabbed the pile of box files and bundled them onto the back seat of her car. Hooking up her phone to the sound system, she set off for her meeting with the solicitor. She didn't know whether it was her heightened emotional state or the alchemy of the inflection of the songs, but her appetite to learn more about this extraordinary music grew stronger the more she listened to it.

The solicitor assigned to deal with probate explained the process for settling the estate. She confirmed that it looked like Sarah was the sole beneficiary of the will. If that turned out to be the case then Sarah would inherit the cottage and her grandfather's savings. The lawyer saw no objection to Sarah continuing to live there. She said she would inform the authorities and utility companies so that Sarah rather than the estate would meet ongoing costs. After the taxman had taken his chunk of her granddad's money and legal fees, she would be left with around £30,000 in cash.

An unexpected feeling of relief washed over Sarah. Until that moment she had not realised the worry she must have been feeling about being homeless and jobless. If her own savings could see her through until this generous inheritance arrived she could buy time to sort out her uncertain future. It seemed to her as though her grandfather was looking out for her in death as he had in life.

As she drove home to the cottage, the lilting music of the lyra accompanied her undulating emotions. Sadness, gratitude, love and loss surged with the cadences and plunged into the silent interstices in the melodies. Tears fell down her cheeks as she drove, not sobs of distress but slow steady tears as she considered what had gone from her life.

She thought of how she owed everything to her grandfather, the man who had selflessly healed her pain, encouraged her to succeed, provided for her in life and now after his death had bequeathed her not only his home and money but a musical instrument which opened up another avenue to follow in her life.

She knew not where it would take her, but she had to set out on that journey to honour him, to 'go on and conquer the world'.

Like a child before a holiday, Sarah hardly slept. Up with the first vestiges of the new dawn she busied herself making breakfast then found she couldn't eat it. She checked directions on her phone then left to catch a train so early she had to find a café in London to drink coffee and restlessly while away the time until her appointment with Yannis.

Tall with long black hair, the young man opened the door to the ground-floor flat in Finchley. His smile put Sarah immediately at her ease but behind his eyes she detected a melancholy.

'*Ella*, come in.' Yannis ushered Sarah into the small apartment that doubled as a studio. Several lyras stood on stands along with a guitar leant against a wall, a violin case on a chair, music stands and other paraphernalia of a musician's trade.

'*Signomi*, I am sorry about the mess, I have so little space here, and it is not home,' said Yannis longingly, clearing a pile of books from a chair and indicating for her to sit down. 'This is your lyra?' He held out his arms for Sarah to pass him the case.

Opening the first catch, Yannis carefully manipulated the other dented clip to release it before he deferentially opened the lid. Sarah noticed the musician's eyes on seeing the lyra had lost their far-away look and reconnected with the present. 'It is beautiful, and quite old I would say?' She said that the instrument could date back to the Second World War.

'That would make sense. Much before that time we had the lyraki, a smaller instrument thought to have developed from the Byzantine lyra first made more than a thousand years ago.' Yannis' face turned serious as he warmed to his theme.

'Although it had three strings the melody was only played on two with the central string used as a drone which resonated with an unchanged note to accompany the tune. This is a common Cretan lyra on which all strings play the melody and was developed just before the war.

'How did you come by this?' questioned Yannis. 'It is unusual to find such an old instrument, particularly in Britain.'

Sarah told him the little that she knew about her grandfather escaping from the Nazis on Crete.

'Then your *pappous* is a hero, he fought to help save our people'.

As Yannis bent to string the instrument, Sarah retold the parts of the story she had gleaned from Douglas on the day of the funeral. When she mentioned that she was a violinist, Yannis explained that he too was studying the instrument in London.

The lyra restrung, the young Cretan rubbed rosin on the bow and drew it across the strings. In his hands, the instrument immediately came alive. He held the arched bow with a finger

62

between the pad and the ancient horse hair which kept breaking away as he played.

'I think the bow has seen better days, it must have deteriorated over the years. Nowadays people tend to use violin bows anyway.'

He took up one of his own bows and resumed playing. Sarah was mesmerised by the freedom expressed in the sound that stretched, bent, repeated and moulded a melody within an inch of its life.

'Here, let's see what you can do.' Yannis handed Sarah her lyra and his bow, before explaining the rudiments of holding both. He told her how the strings are stopped by the player pressing their fingernails against their sides rather than with direct downward pressure.

It took little time for Sarah to understand the basics of how to play the instrument but it was apparent it would take practice to master the technique that was quite different from playing a violin. During the lesson, she managed to play the simple tune Yannis had taught her and the teacher felt sure she would make good progress.

'You are doing well,' encouraged Yannis. 'You're a good musician, you understand. Now it is practice, practice, practice and then you must find the soul of the music. Have you been to Crete?'

Although she had travelled to any number of countries around the world with the orchestra, Sarah had never been to Greece, let alone the most southerly of its archipelago of islands in the eastern Mediterranean.

'The lyra has the spirit of Crete at its core,' explained Yannis. 'To be a great player you must understand the landscape, history, culture of my island and its people. The best musicians have the power to reach out to every Cretan. They can empty their minds of everything but the essence of what it is to be born to that magical island.'

It had started to dawn on Sarah the scope of the challenge she had confronted herself with. What did she want out of the lyra? Why was she so keen to learn it? Was it just curiosity or to honour the memory of her granddad and his untold past? She began to understand that it was something deeper and even more fundamental. She knew she had to learn the instrument, and to achieve what she wanted was a steep mountain to scale.

'Don't worry,' said Yannis, seeing her look of deflation and sensing her apprehension. 'You have much talent. More than that, you are Cretan.'

Her teacher could see Sarah looked puzzled. 'You grandfather, he fought for us in the war,' he smiled. He will always be one of us. He was a brother in arms and, as his granddaughter you too are a child of our island.' He paused.

'You will come back?'

Sarah looked at her watch. The two hours she had booked had already flown past.

'I would like that, if you have time?' she smiled.

'To be honest, I have lots of time. When I am not studying or practicing there is little left for me to do in London. I miss home, to tell you the truth, and having someone to talk to about music and the lyra has made my day. How about tomorrow at one? I am free most afternoons.'

'I'd like that, if you're sure?' She reached in her bag and pulled out £50 and handed it to Yannis. 'And how much do I owe you for the strings?'

'The lessons are on me, your grandfather was a hero.' Yannis held up his hands.

'I can't not pay you, I have the money,' insisted Sarah.

'And I will not take it,' he stubbornly replied.

'Then I cannot come back,' countered Sarah.

Sensing they were reaching an impasse Yannis conceded, 'If you don't mind, in return you could help me with my violin studies?'

Honour satisfied, Sarah capitulated and they agreed to try to meet as often as possible. In the days that followed, she made good progress. She was an attentive student and picked things up quickly. Sarah practiced for hours and in any spare time left, she immersed herself learning about Crete. If she were to be an honorary Cretan it was best she learn a thing or two about her new adoptive homeland.

Knowing nothing about the island, Sarah was drawn in by what she read. Greece's largest island had been separated from the motherland for most of its turbulent history. It was on this island of towering mountain ranges, hidden plateaux and secluded coves that the first Europeans, the Minoans, had settled sometime during the third millennium BCE. Since the demise of that 'cradle of civilisation' in around 1450 BCE the island, sitting as it does at the gateway between Europe, Africa and Asia, became the target for any number of invading armies seeking to exploit its location.

She read that Myceneans, Dorians, mainland Greeks and Romans all occupied the island even before the birth of Christ. Following the split in the Roman Empire, Crete became Byzantine territory before being gifted to the Italian crusader Boniface who promptly sold it to the Venetians in the 13th century.

Some four hundred years later in 1645 AD the Ottoman Turks began their invasion and ultimate occupation of the island, beginning a further period of untold deprivation and Cretan revolt against their cruel overlords. It was not until 1898 that Crete became an independent state and even then it was not united with Greece until 1913. That period of independence was short lived as in 1941, following what at the time was the largest airborne invasion ever mounted, the island was occupied by the Germans and their Italian allies.

It was this terrible chapter in Crete's history which had brought Sarah to where she was now and had indirectly touched her life through her grandfather's experiences in that bitter struggle.

The end of the Second World War saw little respite for the embattled Cretans as the whole of Greece fell into a violent civil war; as if that was not enough, as recently as 1967 a coup by a group of army colonels saw Greece in the hands of a military dictatorship, which lasted for seven years. Even now Crete, along with the rest of Greece, was enduring a debt crisis which was tearing apart its social fabric.

The more she read, the more Sarah found empathy with the deep affection Yannis felt for the island of his birth. After lessons they would adjourn to a pub on the corner of the street and over a drink he would reminisce about his home. Through Yannis and her reading, she began to understand the fierce individuality, generosity and pride that were fundamental to the culture she had been led to discover through the lyra in the attic.

Her progress on the instrument impressed Yannis. The music he gave her to play was like the flying bird chiselled on the body of her instrument. It rose, hovered and swooped and with it Sarah felt she was flying above the Cretan mountains she had read about. In those moments, death and abandonment became subsumed as she

67

became a tiny dot on a faraway hillside beneath that soaring eagle of sound.

As the days passed, Sarah's passion for the lyra grew. Wrapped up in the notes, rhythm and melody of the music was something much more than the sum of those parts. She progressed with her playing and her mind cleared of its initial frenzied excitement. She realised this new-found love might be more than just a way of honouring her grandfather.

Chapter 4

AS THE TWO men left the village of Samaria, the going immediately got harder and was made more challenging for John by the throbbing in his head, a legacy from the previous day's celebrations. The sun began to gather in strength and its effect as it burned through the morning mist could be felt even under the canopy of the trees that clung tenaciously to the rocks. John was pleased to be following his companion, whose sure-footed steps made light work of what would for most have been a formidable climb.

'It is hard to climb after yesterday, but we are not going far,' Vassilis announced. John was reassured that he was not alone in feeling jaded. 'The climb will do us both good.' John took his fellow musician's word for it and as they continued to forge a way across the mountainside the ache in his head lifted with the haze and the soft tinkling of goat bells soothed what remained of his hangover. At last the sun rose high enough to shine down through the gorge and began to fill in the colours of the trees and rocks.

'From the top of the gorge to the sea is sixteen kilometres dropping down 1,250 metres,' said Vassilis. 'If we keep walking up we will reach the plateau of Omalos. But we will not go out on the plain. That is as far as the road from Chania travels and already German troops have found their way there.'

In the splendid isolation of the mountains, it was sobering to recall that nearby lurked the danger of the invading army. It was almost impossible to reconcile the hell that could be wrought with this piece of paradise.

'We got word last night. The Germans are advancing further than we thought. We can control the gorge, I don't think they will risk their troops in this terrain, which we can easily defend. But they have hubris, a Greek word you have in English I think?'

John knew the word but was unsure of its meaning. 'They have conceit, they have the pride to challenge the gods, but in our mythology hubris will lead to their nemesis or downfall. We cannot be sure they will not try to conquer the mountains. They are angry at the way Cretans defend their own land. Already they are seeking reprisals. It is the fear of these that is our biggest enemy. It is best for us to be where nobody knows so tongues cannot be loosened.'

The commando was to some extent reassured by Vassilis' confidence in the impregnability of the gorge, but had seen enough of the German war machine in action not to underestimate the extent of its horrific ambitions.

As the gorge widened they stopped following its course and struck out west, scaling the side of the valley cut through the limestone rock by the river flowing from the White Mountains to the Libyan Sea.

'This river is like the Cretan people, it is gentle and generous but when angry it is strong and defiant. In winter it becomes a raging torrent and it is almost impossible to get in or out of the gorge. This small stream you see created this natural fortress.' Stopping, Vassilis spread his arms wide in a gesture of pride at the wonder of the land around him.

'In the distance are the highest peaks of the White Mountains, the Lefka Ori, they cover about eight hundred square kilometres of the south west of the island.'

John surveyed the view. 'Is there still snow on the tops of the mountains?' he queried, staring at the brilliant white peaks.

'They are called the White Mountains because they never change colour. In winter and spring they are covered in snow but, when that melts, they glow the same white as the sun reflects off their limestone peaks,' explained the young Greek. 'This will be

71

our view from the bedroom window for some time now. Not too bad, is it?'

John would have agreed with his new friend in other circumstances, but the exhilaration he felt at the splendour of what he saw was laced with apprehension at his predicament. Seeing the Englishman's head drop his Greek guide reassured him. 'Not long now, maybe three hours until we reach the hideout.'

They kept up what John considered to be a good speed but he suspected that for Vassilis this was little more than strolling pace. Every now and then he caught glimpses of the sea glimmering through the trees to the south. Much of the way they walked single file, but when the terrain allowed they walked side by side in companionship.

Their immediate chat was of the battle and what Vassilis knew about the occupation. He explained that some of the retreating troops had left weapons for the Cretan Resistance and that, like John, there were other Allied soldiers fugitive in the hills. It was early days yet, but a network of runners was already set up carrying messages from leaders across the island and the Resistance movement was gaining strength. When Vassilis had exhausted all he knew about the war they talked of happier days, before the invasion.

Inevitably, the conversation turned to music, and Vassilis related how he was the son of a musician who played lyra at weddings, concerts, dances and other gatherings across the island. To supplement his income his father was also a lyra maker, crafting instruments from timber sourced from the forests. His small workshop was in the ancient streets that squirreled out from the harbour side of the city of Chania to the north, near to where John had come ashore and now overrun by German troops.

The family home was in a village to the south of the city where, like many Cretans, they owned some olive trees and grazed a flock of goats on the mountainside. Vassilis had learned to play the lyra at his father's knee and was much in demand throughout the west of the island, and travelling far and wide sometimes on foot, sometimes with his donkey, to perform. He too hoped to become a luthier and the lyra now slung across his back was the result of his first attempt with the help of his father.

Unlike Vassilis, John's family had no interest in music. His father was a farm labourer whose only exposure to it came with an occasional singsong in the village pub. John's passion had been sparked indirectly through a school friend, the son of a wealthy family who he had met at school when he was eleven years old. His friend's parents owned a portable wind-up gramophone and a collection of brittle 78 rpm records which the boys would spend hours listening to.

The family had bought the boy a violin and every week he would reluctantly attend lessons given by a private tutor who would come to their house. The son would rather have been out playing cricket, rugby or football and made little progress, but his young friend, without any tuition, would pick up the instrument and fashion a tune.

Impressed by the sounds emanating from his drawing room one day his friend's father opened the door only to find it was John rather than his son who was playing. It was decided that the boy would relinquish his instrument to his friend who continued to teach himself. At school John impressed with his prowess and a music teacher took up his cause and provided the young protégé with free lessons when he could. His musical ability and academic progress saw John get a letter of acceptance to study at the Royal College of Music just months before the outbreak of war.

'Now we are home,' declared Vassilis, suddenly John looked around him for any sign of shelter. 'You can't see anything? That is good.'

Parting the foliage between two bushes like a curtain, Vassilis beckoned John to follow, and entering a fissure in the mountainside he slipped out of sight. John barely squeezed through after his guide. On the other side the crevice opened into a huge cave. From the ground stalagmites rose up looking for all the world like broken columns fashioned by some god to support the natural vaulted ceiling that soared above. Already goatskins had been laid out over beds of straw, and wood had been set in a makeshift fire at the centre of the cavern.

'We even have running water,' Vassilis pointed to the back of the cave where a narrow tunnel dropped down into the bowels of the mountain. In the silence John could make out the murmur of a spring finding its way through the cracks in the rocks that engulfed them.

The cool walls of the cave brought a welcome relief from the heat. Vassilis unpacked a feast of cold meat left over from the wedding, hard rusks that he poured wine on to soften and topped with roughly chopped tomatoes and soft, creamy mizithra cheese.

As night fell the two men lit the fire and settled down to drink wine and exchange experiences from their past. Again their love of music came to the fore and Vassilis took his lyra from the case and passed it to John, explaining the intricacies of how he had crafted it and telling him a little of the instrument's history.

'The timber I used to make this lyra was collected before I was born. The wood for the body needs to be at least ten years old but my father collected this from the walnut trees in Spili more than twenty years ago. The soundboard comes from much older wood. He transported by donkey the wooden joists from a wreck of a Venetian house in Rethymnon. They were more than three hundred years old, and the one I used to carve the face of this instrument is cedar.

75

'It is the soundboard that is really important to the tone. Until this war I would collect wood for father on my travels and he stores it to age, so in ten years or so I hope I will be making instruments with the wood I have collected. You are lucky, Captain John,' laughed Vassilis. 'My lyra is of the new design which has been influenced by the fiddle and will be easier for you to play.'

The young Cretan explained how until recently the music of the island had been played predominantly either on a violin or a lyraki, a smaller lyra. Often the bow would be strung with bells providing the accompaniment.

'This lyra is modern and all the strings can be used so the range is much larger and I can play a more extensive repertoire. We have mated the lyraki and the fiddle to give birth to a Cretan lyra which still has its roots in our past. Many luthiers carve a double-headed eagle on the back of the body, an allusion to its Byzantine heritage I think. It is also symbolic of the Orthodox Church in my country. I am not so religious. To me music is my religion, I carved a golden eagle, which soars and swoops like the music of my island and is free.' Vassilis handed the lyra to John who turned it over to look at the beautiful bird, the relief carving of an eagle chiselled out of the curved back of the body. He ran his hands gently over the feathers, head, beak and talons so lovingly etched in the oiled walnut.

Turning the instrument over, it was clear that it was the work of a master craftsman and created with love. Seeing John's appreciation of his lyra Vassilis explained, 'My father is a perfectionist, every evening he would examine my work and if it was not just right he would help me to make it so. To me it plays well. I hope I can make more instruments for other musicians when the war is over.'

John plucked at a string. 'It is beautiful.'

His friend moved to sit beside him. 'Let me show you.'

Vassilis demonstrated simple scales, stopping the strings to the side with the long fingernails on his left hand. He then passed the lyra to John and showed him how to hold the bow. At first, although he immediately mastered the fingering of the scales, his hands found it difficult to unlearn the automatic discipline of stopping the strings by pressing down on them. Once he began to teach his fingers to adapt to this new way of playing his progress was fast and on that first evening in the cave he learned to play his first simple song.

The two men fell into a routine. Each day Vassilis would leave the cave for hours and return with food and drink from remote villages miles distant. Whilst he was away, John would sit and practice on the lyra the lessons he had been taught by his friend the night before. When immersed in playing he could forget the war raging throughout the world outside the cave. Within the confines of their hideout the music he played took on greater resonance as it echoed off the damp walls giving it the power to evoke images of the wild landscape outside the mouth of their mountain refuge.

Occasionally Vassilis would go out for the night taking his lyra with him to play at a gathering. Alone without the instrument for company, the young soldier would feel the full weight of his situation like water pressing down on a deep-sea diver. On such evenings, John would sit outside the entrance to the cave beneath the covering of trees that masked their lair, enjoying the warmth of the summer sun.

As the weeks went by, Vassilis returned to the cave with stories of life outside; of the awful atrocities, the murder of women and children by an occupying force angry that they couldn't subdue this brave people. John began to notice that the rations Vassilis brought back were becoming more slender and although the lyra player made no mention of any shortages John pressed him to tell the truth.

As the Axis troops established themselves on the island, Vassilis told John, they were requisitioning all the food they needed from villagers, leaving local people to survive on the little they could hide. The Royal Navy blockade of the island was creating shortages for the occupying army that made the situation worse for the starving Cretans. Although the Germans did not dare risk entering the Samaria Gorge the villagers there were under siege as there were enemy units posted on the Omalos Plateau at its head. The locals would take in what they could by boat but the Germans controlled many of the surrounding coastal villages from where supplies could be shipped.

Autumn went and winter descended, the snows providing an additional defensive curtain around the hideout but also making Vassilis' expeditions to forage for wild greens, nuts and berries a gargantuan task. The distance he could travel to source supplies was severely limited. To help find food it was agreed that on some days John would leave the cave to forage near their hideout whilst Vassilis would go further afield.

Although he had to break cover, leaving the cave was a liberation for John. Some days all he could see was a sea of dazzling white as though a starched counterpane had been thrown over the mountainside. Occasionally he would catch glimpses of the Aegean Sea the tone of pure blue almost as unimaginable as escape to the safety of Africa which lay on its southern shoreline.

When the snows melted, the mountains both inside and outside the cave became alive with the sound of water rushing over and through the rocks to the sea thousands of feet below. These days were good as Vassilis could hike further afield in search of food and John could forage for snails and horta, the wild greens which dotted the mountainside. But pickings were slim and news from the wider world was not good. Most of the population were starving and lived in fear of the atrocities increasingly meted out by the enemy. The German high command had instructed their troops to show no mercy to the Cretans whose proud defiance spurred their oppressors on to even greater feats of inhumanity. The rough winter seas severely curtailed the already dangerous missions to smuggle supplies to the bottom of the gorge from along the coast.

John was now unrecognisable from the young soldier who had landed at Souda Bay the previous summer. Heavily bearded, with long hair his body grew leaner as the shortage of food took its toll. Although at times he felt the pangs of hunger, Vassilis always managed to return with something for them to eat, however meagre. John looked forward to the evenings when the two men would light a fire inside the cave and sit and play the lyra. Somehow, the music was a symbol of hope, a talisman temporarily exorcising the evil that pervaded the world outside.

All this time however, the Resistance was getting more organised. Towards the end of that winter Vassilis brought news that some radio sets had been smuggled onto the island and a network to help fugitive soldiers escape was being established. They learned that just a month after the surrender two British submarines had liberated 200 troops who were being sheltered by the monks at Preveli Monastery far to the east but that escape route had been closed down as it was now too dangerous.

There was still hope, though. Operating out of Egypt the Royal Navy was still running vessels under cover of darkness to Crete to liberate soldiers like John who were on the run, and to drop special troops, arms and radios to help the Resistance. Vassilis was upbeat.

'We must be patient. My unit is in touch with the network. They know you are here. There is a radio and an operator hiding out near Sougia, twenty kilometres along the coast to the west, so we are in contact with the British now. With any luck when the storms of winter are over they will resume operations.'

As winter passed into spring the men were getting weaker, it seemed that every day John would have to pull the rope around the waist of his baggy shepherd's trousers tighter and the coarse vest just hung off his body. For both men the paltry food they could scavenge from the mountainside kept their bodies together but the music they played through the dark evenings nourished their spirit. Vassilis had proved to be an excellent teacher and John a talented pupil. The music was not just a welcome diversion to their day-to-day lives but the thing that made their lives worth living. The emotional power created through the lyra allowed them, momentarily at least, to transcend the fear of the dangers they faced.

The word came in late March, the Royal Navy were to attempt a rescue from the beach at the base of the Gorge of Tripitis. For the two men, making the rendezvous would be risky as they would have to leave behind the security provided by the Samaria Gorge and skirt the Omalos Plateau to pick up a trail to Mount Gigilos, which they would need to climb to find the entrance to the gorge. Once there, the descent would be tough but there were many hiding places.

'It is ideal,' reassured Vassilis, 'The gorge is named after the Greek word *tripes* which means holes, there are plenty of caves there where we can shelter. I will get you to the beach, no worry.'

The pick-up from Tripitis was scheduled for a week's time. They decided to make an early start to return to the village of Samaria then travel under cover of darkness stopping to sleep during the day. Although Vassilis appeared confident of getting John to the beach, he was aware the journey involved a serious element of risk. The network reported that the Germans had deployed specially trained units to track down Resistance fighters and Allied troops still hiding in the mountains. The Cretans had the advantage of knowing the lie of the land and had men who could defend the entrances to Samaria Gorge but once away from the safety of the canyon they would likely be on their own.

As they began their descent from the cave towards Samaria, spring sun seeped through the canopy of pines and cypresses, its benign warmth belying the dangers that lay ahead. The two men were in buoyant mood; John in particular was filled with the anticipation of being reunited with people in the village after ten months of isolation, and with adrenaline at the planned escape to Egypt.

They were welcomed with a spread of food that for months they could only have dreamed of. It was clear to John this was not the usual recent fare of the villagers who, compared to when he had last seen them, were shadows of their former selves. Their smiling faces were sunken and etched with the struggle they were enduring. This show of hospitality towards him touched him deeply. Eggs, bread, eels and freshwater crabs accompanied olive paste and horta, and toasts to freedom were made in wine and raki.

The warmth of early spring had coaxed the aromas of wild herbs from the hillsides. The food, the sun and the hospitality of the villagers made it easy for John to forget the dangers that lay ahead. He tried to put aside thoughts of that uncertain future and live in that unforgettable moment.

Vassilis was encouraged to take out his lyra and he played as he had never played before, as if there were no tomorrow. As his fingers moved and he drew his bow across the strings he became as one with the lyra, which in turn became a part of all that surrounded them. The valleys and hills and the brave, hospitable people were subsumed in that magical moment as John looked upwards at the mountains they would soon have to climb. As he stared into the clear blue of the sky the shadow of a golden eagle hovered against the white orb of the sun.

When the music finished there was an awestruck silence before applause rippled around the gathering. Vassilis stood and held his arms out wide his lyra in one hand, the bow in the other, accepting the generous adulation. He walked towards John still holding out the instrument and it was then that the entranced soldier realised he was holding the lyra for him.

'Play, maestro,' whispered the young Greek. 'You might never get the chance again.'

The applause abated, the villagers not knowing what to expect. John tentatively eased the bow across the strings, relying on the hours of solitary practice in the cave for his fingers to find the notes. And the melody came, as if conjured from the ether. John let his instinct take over and his confidence mounted as the tempo increased. The music, the mountains and the gathered villagers became one as his playing became more febrile. Shouts of '*Opa!*' rang out from the audience, astounded at the virtuosity of this foreigner who could play lyra. John knew his playing stood no comparison to that of his friend but it was more than competent and like the young luthier captured the spirit of that moment in the mountains. The song finished, the applause was generous and heartfelt, and John handed the lyra back to the master.

'Thank you for your hospitality, and *kefi*, your love of life, long may it continue.' Vassilis raised a glass of raki. 'Your kindness will always be remembered. I will play one more song and then we must rest. We leave tonight.'

John slept fitfully as Vassilis snored loudly on the straw bed next to his. His head was filled with the elation he had felt at being able to play music to an audience again and apprehension about the coming days. It felt as though he had just fallen asleep when he was roused by his companion.

The village was in darkness as the two men slipped out of the cottage in which they had spent the night. John noticed that across his back Vassilis now carried a rifle as well as his lyra. He searched for his own service revolver and stuffed it in his waistband. In idle moments in the cave he had stripped and cleaned the weapon for which he only had a few rounds of ammunition left. Passing the church of Agios Nikolaos, John remembered the wedding on those first days following his escape. It seemed an eternity away and he wondered, if he evaded capture, how he would ever be able to thank the Cretans for the kindness they had shown him. From here the going got steeper as the two men followed a rock-strewn track towards the mouth of the canyon.

A whistle broke the silence. Holding up his arm Vassilis stopped his climb and listened. The whistle came again, this time the young Greek responded.

The shadow of a large man stepped out from behind a rock, two rifles strapped across his back and a handgun and fearsome dagger tucked in the cummerbund wrapped around his waist. John made little sense of the whispered conversation between the men but the lookout bade them onwards with wishes of '*sto kalo, kalo taxidi*'.

They had reached Xyloskalo at the head of the gorge. The guard had told Vassilis that there were Germans billeted in the village of Omalos a few kilometres away. The path to the mountain started not far away. John felt his breath quicken as they emerged onto the plateau.

'Get down.' An urgent whisper from his friend urged John to the ground behind a wall just in time as a pair of German soldiers passed by on the other side. In a heightened state of awareness, the two men crossed the short distance to the track that led to the mountain, adrenaline pumping at how close they had come to capture. From here on Vassilis tried to reassure his friend, their passage should be safer, for the time being at least.

The men climbed in silence, concentrating on the treacherous going underfoot. At times John dropped onto all fours to scramble over rocks. Three hours after they had left Samaria Gorge Vassilis stopped and pointed upwards at the summit of the mountain.

'This is Gigilos, the Throne of Zeus,' announced Vassilis. 'I hope he doesn't mind sharing as we will stop here and rest during the daylight hours and head into Tripitis Gorge tomorrow night.'

Vassilis led the way to a tumbledown, abandoned sheep fold from which they could keep watch and find shade. As the sun rose they took it in turns to sleep whilst the other man kept lookout. During his waking hours John wondered at the majesty of nature that surrounded him. Under the cloudless sky he could see down into the narrow, tree-lined gorge that they would follow to the coast. In the distance was the cobalt blue sea that he hoped would carry him to the safety of Egypt.

As evening came, the two men ate the food provided for them by the villagers in Samaria before shouldering their loads and heading towards the Gorge of Tripitis. The rocks suddenly encroached on them and they had to remove their packs before Vassilis could squeeze between the gap at the entrance to the canyon. John threw the gun, packs and the precious lyra to his friend before passing between the rocks himself.

Vassilis told John that if he felt up to it they would try to make the bottom of the gorge that night and then hole up for the four days before the rescue attempt. He explained that there were other escapees trying to make the rendezvous so the more groups that were operating around the time of the planned landing the more likely they were to draw attention from German troops.

The going was slow in the dark, the Englishman now saw the wisdom in having plenty of time in hand before his escape attempt.

Although treacherous, John had the time to make his descent carefully and without any added pressure.

The cave Vassilis chose was a scramble up the side of the ravine, beneath a rock face the other side of which dropped down to a path which led to the beach of Tripitis a couple of kilometres distant. Clinging to stunted tree trunks and scrub they reached the entrance. The cave was small with just enough room for the two men to lie down and store their packs. The space was too confined to light a fire and they did not want to draw attention to their whereabouts by lighting one outside on the ledge, but they had food that could be eaten cold and fresh water from a stream at the bottom of the canyon.

The next day the men slept well following their climb but their waking hours dragged. The lyra stayed in its case and conversation was held in hushed tones. Vassilis told John that on the evening of the rendezvous he would escort him to the beach. If all had gone to plan a message would have been sent to Egypt that the soldiers were near the coast and awaiting rescue. The night in question would be moonless and a fast motor launch would anchor off the coast and send a tender in to ferry the men to the vessel. The approaching small craft would signal with a light and at the response of a whistle would come ashore. Any who did not make it to the beach would be left behind. The pickup was to be at 9.00pm to give the escapees time to reach the beach under cover of darkness and for the ship to have time to put distance between it and the coast before the following morning.

The afternoon before the rendezvous the men ate then stashed their sparse belongings in their packs. As the sun dropped below the peaks of the White Mountains they stepped out onto the ledge outside the cave. Vassilis would climb first scaling the six metres of rock face leading to the summit and the path to the coast. He made the climb look easy and, just short of the top, turned and signalled to John to follow in his footsteps.

The shot missed Vassilis by a metre but was enough to loosen the boulders above his head. The rocks crashing down hit his leg with enough force to knock him from the mountainside back onto the ledge below. John instinctively reached for his revolver and could now see in the half-light the helmets of several enemy soldiers taking cover further up the ravine.

Vassilis' leg had been shattered, either by the falling rock or by the impact of the drop. He levered himself into a sitting position on the ledge and John could see his friend's face lined with pain. Unshouldering his rifle, the Resistance fighter took aim and fired a shot, pinning the lead soldier back behind a rock.

'Quick, you must go now. I can cover you from here for some time,' the young Cretan said. He reached for his bottle of raki and took a large slug. *Eleftheria y thanatos*, this will numb the pain,' he tried a smile.

The irony was not lost on John but he was reluctant to leave his friend. Vassilis urged him, 'Go now or the whole operation will be at risk. I can hold them off from here and maybe kill a few; they do not know which way you are heading. *Kalo taxidi*.'

In that moment which seemed to John like an eternity, Vassilis reached down and handed him his lyra. 'Now go. Play for me.'

'*Efharisto*, thank you.' Moved beyond belief, it was all John could think to say. Another shot rang out from Vassilis' gun covering the Englishman as he made the ascent to the top of the cliff face. At the summit he took a moment to look down at this man he would never forget; a smile on his face, a bottle of raki by his side and a gun at his shoulder.

'*Adio, Vassilis. Eleftheria y thanatos*.' Knocked back by the impact of a bullet ricocheting off the rock, lying on the ground John searched for any sign of injury before noticing the dented catch on the music case that had taken the deflection. Raising his head, he spotted the track just where his friend had said it would be, and headed for the beach. Single shots were returned by salvos of gunfire ringing out from the other side of the escarpment, then quiet. John knew it was over for his brave comrade.

Several hundred metres on, the commando left the track and found cover in the rocks which fell away to the sea. If the Germans followed, the operation would be in jeopardy. He had no watch and tried to count what he estimated was half an hour. Still no enemy

90

troops passed. He had to go now if he was to make the rendezvous. Cautiously breaking cover he regained the path towards the shore.

Chapter 5

HER SOLICITOR MADE clear that dealing with probate and the taxman would probably take a year. All Sarah would need to provide her lawyer with was a realistic valuation of the property for the Revenue.

Never having been frivolous and despite some recent expenditure on wedding preparations, Sarah still had funds in the bank. For the time being at least, she did not have to worry about money or putting a roof over her head. Despite this, a feeling of disquiet blocked her road to recovery from the hurt she had suffered. Only when she picked up the lyra did she feel complete, emptying her mind of anxieties the recent past had brought to bear.

Without the lyra she was lost. The only company she sought was Yannis'. When they were not together or she was not playing,

Sarah felt the weight of loneliness pressing down on her. In the past, her grandfather had always been there for her, and before his unfaithfulness, she had found happiness with Gareth. But she could never go back to a man who had betrayed her so badly. The fact that he had been too cowardly to respond to her text message spoke volumes about him.

Alone in the cottage, awareness of her isolation would descend. When the fog of depression swept down, Sarah realised how much of herself she had invested in Gareth and her career. Surely, there had been a life before him? Was it possible the only relationships she had left were with ex-work colleagues in an orchestra now hundreds of miles away in Europe?

Of course, she told herself, she had had friends. Thinking back the three years before she had met the handsome record company executive she had known other people. It now felt a lifetime ago that they had met at the launch party for a recording of Vaughan Williams' pieces on which she had performed.

What a fool she had been. Sarah had told herself that long working hours made it difficult to maintain old friendships but, in reality, she had allowed herself to become part of Gareth's life. Eventually her phone had stopped ringing; her career and relationship with one man became her world.

When not working they had found time to meet his friends. She hadn't worried when her fiancé went out to play tennis on

Sunday morning, returning after lunchtime in the pub. This was Sarah's time to spend visiting her granddad. Looking back, she could now see how Gareth had cut her off from her previous life. At best he had been selfish, at worst controlling.

In that moment of clarity she recalled life before Gareth, friends from college and school and brief relationships with other men. Among the pile of her papers, books and magazines she had stacked in the study was her address book. Flicking through the crossings out and loose change of address cards stuffed between its pages she found the number she was looking for.

Her hand poised holding her mobile, Sarah hesitated. Any confidence she had drained away as the 'what ifs?' started to cloud her resolve. If she did not dial now, the anxiety would get worse. Clearing her head of all thoughts as to what she was going to say she dialled, and pressed call.

When Liz answered, the years dropped away. There was no retribution for their neglected relationship, just an eagerness to catch up on their lives since they last met more than three years before. Since Sarah had started secondary school the two girls had been there for each other; problems at home, with boys and the stress of exams were all lighter when shared between them. Even now, just talking made Sarah feel better. It was as though the two old friends were back at school.

Eager to get together and make up for lost time, the two women realised they still lived locally and arranged to meet that evening. Sarah decided to walk the two miles to the pub. Instead of the anxiety she thought she might feel, she tingled with anticipation at connecting with Liz again.

As she walked, Sarah remembered the days before she had met Gareth when barely a week went by without meeting her friend. Liz had always been the strong one who knew her own mind and would support Sarah whenever she needed it. When she first got together with her ex fiancé, Liz had called numerous times to invite the couple for drinks, to dinner or even to meet up for a coffee. Somehow, Gareth always had a reason not to go, and eventually Liz stopped calling.

On walking into the dark-beamed saloon bar, in an instant Sarah recognised her friend sitting in an armchair at a low table by the welcoming log fire. As she approached, the tall, blonde haired woman stood before bending down to hug her petite friend. In each other's eyes, the two women had not changed a bit. As they hugged, Sarah felt as though she was reconnecting with life.

They gave each other space to talk about the last few years, and reminisced about schooldays, their respective colleges and jobs, Sarah talking about the orchestra and Liz about her work as a development chef for a chain of supermarkets. After several glasses of wine, the friends tried to apologise for losing contact both claiming it to be their fault, although Liz could see that Sarah still carried a burden of guilt.

'There's no blame, life just got in the way. Let's put it behind us. We're together now,' reassured Liz, squeezing her friend's hand across the table.

Neither of them wanted the evening to end. With drinking up time called, they ordered a cab to go to the cottage. Sarah had told her friend about the lyra and, as they sat in the lounge, was encouraged by Liz to play.

'It always did annoy me, that you could pick up any musical instrument and within no time be able to play it,' Liz joked. 'That is so beautiful.'

Sarah spoke with passion about the instrument, her lessons with Yannis, and what she had been told by Douglas about her grandfather's past in Crete.

'I went there on holiday last year,' revealed Liz. 'With my boyfriend at the time, we went to a place called Agia Pelagia, somewhere on the north coast I think it was. Anyway, that's what split us up. It was lovely, and I wanted to see more of the island, but he just wanted to lounge around on the beach drinking beer. We had a row; I hired a car, drove west into the mountains. We met up at the airport for the flight home and haven't spoken since.'

'I'm sorry, that sounds dreadful,' said Sarah.

'Not at all, I had a great time. It was best we found out that we didn't like the same things before getting in too deep. Anyway, I loved the island and would like to go back sometime if I get a chance. You playing the lyra somehow took me there again.

'Why don't you go? After all, your teacher said that you were a Cretan? Go and find out what it's all about.'

As Liz talked about the island, her suggestion began to make sense. There was nothing to keep Sarah in England. She could do with a holiday and some sun. It occurred to the young musician that the two things that had preoccupied her recently had been her grandfather's death and the lyra he had left for her in the loft. Perhaps discovering more about his story would help her come to terms with the past. Her granddad had looked after her in life, perhaps following the story of the lyra he had bequeathed could help ease her grief now.

Late into the night they trawled the internet for package deals to Crete. Sarah had no idea where to start. In that moment, with her friend there to brace her confidence she took the plunge and booked a flight to Athens. There she could at least visit the Parthenon before catching a flight to Crete's capital Heraklion. She could find accommodation as she travelled. This would give her freedom to go wherever the story led her.

Riding the tube to Finchley the following day, Sarah began to have doubts about the wisdom of her plan as fortitude deserted her.

97

Her teacher was enthusiastic when she revealed the news of her trip, and assured Sarah that she would be fine travelling alone and have no problem finding places to stay in early springtime.

'Crete is a large island. It would help if you had a clue where to start your journey,' he advised.

'I know nothing about my granddad's time there during the war. I really don't know where to start. I just need to get away. Maybe I'll just see where the journey takes me.'

'In that case your journey will be easy, there is plenty to see: Knossos, Spinalonga, Samaria Gorge, Lassithi, Vai... You could even take a boat to Santorini – but I think you want... No, I think you need more than that. What about the old soldier you told me about at the funeral, Douglas? Couldn't he give you a place to start?' suggested Yannis.

'He said my grandfather was very reluctant to talk about his past, even to him. I suppose I could try.' She paused.

'Wait. Douglas did mention he had contacted my granddad's old regiment to find out about his medal. Perhaps they could at least tell me where on the island he had fought?'

Calling Douglas that evening, she found him full of encouragement about her plan to visit Crete, and he promised to try and find contact details for his friend's regiment. True to his word, within the hour he had called back with a number.

'They were very helpful,' remembered Douglas. 'But that was a long time ago. Good luck, I hope it helps.'

Only a week before her flight, anything that gave shape to her impulsive journey would help. The next morning Sarah dialled the number Douglas had given her. The archivist could not have been more helpful, and promised to find out what he could, and put any information in the post to Sarah.

To her amazement, the following day an envelope dropped through the letterbox with a letter giving a brief outline of her granddad's service record. The archivist hoped the information would be of use as her trip was imminent. A more detailed history, he wrote, would take longer to piece together due to the nature of her grandfather's service.

She read that following officer training at the start of the Second World War, John Piper had taken a commission in the Royal Artillery. Not long after passing out he had volunteered and been accepted to join one of the first commando units formed in 1940. The next year his unit became part of a special group called Layforce, named after its commander Colonel Robert Laycock.

On the night of the 26th May 1941, the commandos went ashore at Souda Bay on Crete to the east of Chania. The offensive role that had originally been intended for the unit was soon abandoned as the Allied army were already in retreat and Layforce were ordered to provide cover for troops heading south through the White Mountains to Chora Sfakion on the south coast.

For four days, under constant bombardment and air attack, they held the invading Germans at bay, eventually retreating through the Imbros Gorge to Chora Sfakion. By the time they reached the beaches, the operation to evacuate Crete was all but over. Some of the unit made it onto the last ship to leave but of the 800 commandos sent to Crete, less than 200 made it off the island. The others were either killed, taken prisoner or left, like John, to their own devices.

It was not until March the following year that it became clear that the young captain was still at large and along with a number of other soldiers hiding out on the island he was evacuated by a motor launch of the Royal Navy from Tripitis beach on 3rd April 1942. He was then taken via Alexandria to Cairo.

By this time, Layforce had been disbanded. After a period of recuperation, John Piper had moved to the Canal Zone around Suez for specialist training before being assigned to the new Special Air Service. He parachuted in behind enemy lines prior to the D Day landings in June 1944. He won the Military Cross for bravery under enemy fire, in an action that saw him sustain injuries to his arm, which led to its subsequent amputation. He returned to England for a period of rehabilitation and was demobilised in March 1945.

Dumbfounded by her grandfather's story, Sarah could only silently agree with Yannis' assessment that he had been a hero. Neither was she surprised that he had kept quiet about his war years. The mental scars these events must have caused for most would have been unbearable. Sarah's sadness at her granddad's history was suffused with pride in the incredible man who had brought her up.

If her granddad had refused to tell his story, flushed with elation Sarah was eager to share what she had discovered. She phoned Douglas to tell him what she had found out before contacting Liz. Agreeing to meet at the pub the following evening to try to put more flesh on the bones of her adventure, Sarah decided to invite Yannis to help with the planning of her impending trip.

Arriving first, Sarah was waiting at the bar when Liz arrived. They ordered a bottle of wine and, getting an extra glass for Yannis, sat at the low table beside the roaring fire. A few minutes later the lyra teacher arrived.

'Are you OK with wine or would you like something different?' asked Sarah.

'Wine is perfect for me,' replied Yannis, as Liz poured out a glass.

Moving their drinks aside, Yannis spread a map across the table. Drawing rings around the places mentioned in the letter, the young Cretan wrote their names in English so Sarah could read them. He added other locations he thought interesting, particularly the Samaria Gorge that had been used as a hideout by the Resistance, due to its impregnability. By the time Liz had chipped in with places she had enjoyed, the map was covered in blue circles and Sarah's list of places to visit was so long that she was pleased she had not booked a return flight.

The remaining four days went so quickly that Sarah didn't have time to feel the apprehension that was nestling somewhere deep inside her. She had two more lessons with Yannis. The rest of the time had been spent shopping, exchanging currency, getting insurance and booking a hotel in Athens for her overnight stop.

Liz offered to drop her at Heathrow. By the time she had checked in for her flight and got through security there was barely a moment for a coffee before boarding. After a snack, Sarah closed her eyes and slept. When she awoke it was to a clear sky. Through the aircraft window she could see the islands of Croatia afloat on a perfect ultramarine sea, the tiny shape of a yacht painting a white line across its perfect canvas. Soon she caught her first sight of Greece. The plane followed the narrow channel between Albania and the island of Corfu as the pilot announced the start of their descent into Athens.

The heat slapped Sarah in the face as she left the air-conditioned comfort of the airport. Car horns blared as traffic

102

outside the terminal jostled for position. The noise and the fumes were disconcerting but the hint of an aroma of herbs drifted through the polluted air. Tired after the flight, she found her way to the taxi rank and loaded her precious instrument cases into a pristine Mercedes. The hotel in Plaka had been a good choice. Checking in to her room, she showered and, feeling refreshed, headed for the web of narrow streets that meander through the most ancient part of Athens that underlies the Acropolis.

Sarah stopped to catch her breath as she climbed the steep steps. Ascending through the streets, tables spilt out of tavernas, early-flowering plants of every colour bloomed on balconies and in pots placed on the pavements. Reaching the top of the hill, looking up at the Parthenon, Sarah was awestruck at the thought of how the Doric columns that supported the temple had stood on this spot for nearly two-and-a-half millennia. Turning around, Athens was spread out beneath her. Wearing just a T-shirt she was hot in the spring sunshine and wondered at people wearing jumpers and jackets.

Paying to enter the site, she spent extra to join an English-speaking tour. Her guide spoke with passion about Greece's campaign to have the Parthenon Marbles, parts of the frieze that crowned the temple, repatriated to Greece from the British Museum. Walking the stone floors and between the pillars of this venerable symbol of democracy whetted her appetite for a visit to the nearby Acropolis Museum. Most of the artefacts dug from the earth on this ancient hillside were exhibited in this stunning modern building.

Sarah found the museum beautiful. Flooded with light through its giant plate glass windows she felt the dominant presence of the Parthenon which, looking upwards could almost always be seen from inside. Beneath her feet, a glass floor revealed ruins of ancient Athens discovered when the museum was built. She wandered through galleries housing a wealth of votive statues to the goddess Athena, young women their hair braided, carrying gifts of fruit, wreathes and birds; a lion eating a bull; a young man carrying a calf; and warriors on horseback. In the atrium on the top floor she could get up close to the remaining Parthenon marbles, the pieces stolen by Elgin poignantly replaced with plaster replicas.

The abundance of exhibits was overwhelming. Sarah felt that she did not have the time to do them justice. Yannis had told her that there were a formidable number of ancient sites and museums to explore on Crete. She was relieved that with no restraint of time on her journey there, at least, she would be able to do such places justice.

Drifting through the shady streets of Plaka, Sarah relished the warmth, and drank in the sights and sounds of the ancient capital. Stopping for iced coffee, she savoured the sweet, refreshing drink as she swirled the ice with her straw and watched the world go by before resuming her explorations. It amazed her that she could stumble across so many sites of such immense archaeological interest, in this city that had occupied this space on earth for more than 7,000 years.

She strolled the pillars of the Roman Marketplace and marvelled at the Tower of the Winds and the Gate of Athena Archegetis as her mind tried to comprehend the ancient civilisations that had inhabited the very place where she was now standing. Beside the Roman Agora, she came across the Museum of Folk Musical Instruments, housed over the three floors of a 19th century mansion.

Sarah wandered around exhibits of instruments of all kinds, bouzoukis, laoutos, drums and an askomantoura, bagpipes made from a goatskin, and of course lyras. Using the headphones provided, for an hour or so she was able to immerse herself in the music of Greece, until she was reluctantly ushered out of the building at closing time.

Settling on an outside table of a taverna close to her hotel, Sarah realised she had not eaten since that snack on the plane nearly ten hours earlier. The menu was written in both Greek and English, but she was unsure what many of the dishes were. The waiter was happy to help, but when she tried to order a starter and a main course, he suggested that would be far too much food. Maybe she should try a selection of small dishes or *mezzes*.

The plates of hot and cold food kept arriving and Sarah wondered how large what she had considered ordering might have been. Sardines, rusks loaded with oil and tomatoes, cheeses, calamari, spinach pies, zucchini flowers, dolmades, taramasalata, beans, salad and bread, the list was an endless accompaniment to the carafe of ice-cold white wine Sarah sipped as she contentedly whittled away at her first evening in Greece. She could have stayed there for ever had it not been for her sensible side telling her she had to catch an early flight to Crete in the morning.

Waking in the half dawn, the confidence Sarah had felt the night before at being all alone in a foreign land had all but deserted her. She had to force herself from bed and get ready to take a taxi to the airport.

Athens was coming alive in the early morning sunshine. Café owners were busy serving coffee and shopkeepers raised the shutters on their businesses, hosing down the pavements in front of their premises. The streets already busy with cars noisily navigating the narrow streets, Sarah clenched her hands across her lap as her driver responded to the challenge of getting his passenger to the airport.

He could have spared her the anxiety of the nail-biting ride. On arrival at the domestic terminal, notices informing passengers that all flights were cancelled due to industrial action brought Sarah up short. Unsettled by the confusion, she accepted a refund and found her way to the stop for the bus to the ferry terminal in Piraeus, where she had been assured she could get an overnight crossing to Heraklion.

The air-conditioned comfort on the coach came as a relief as she placed her holdall under the seat and cradled the two instrument cases on her lap. The bus travelled at a more leisurely pace than her earlier taxi and Sarah had more time to take in the workaday suburbs of the city.

The picturesque streets of Plaka seemed a long way from the roads she now travelled. The bus pushed its way through the western outskirts of a city that here showed the extent of the deprivation it was suffering under the economic crisis; boarded up businesses and graffitied walls played host to any number of people sleeping rough. Desolate districts cheek by jowl with leafy avenues lined with pooled villas made uncomfortable neighbours as the bus headed for the coast.

In the distance, Sarah caught sight of the unfathomable blue of the sea. There was something about the light, unlike anything she had experienced before, as though some ancient deity had flicked a celestial switch, changing everything. Turning onto the coast road through the exclusive resort of Glyfada, the seafront was lined with expensive restaurants, bars and a marina, but it was the sea that held her attention, the way it segued into a perfect blue sky. Yachts slipped their moorings feeling their way out into the Aegean, heeling to the slightest of breezes blowing onshore.

As the bus swung into the port at Piraeus, Sarah found the size of the harbour daunting. Through the chaos, she identified signs indicating that she was near the terminal for the overnight departure for Heraklion. The bus driver pointed her in the direction of a shipping agency in Plateia Kariaskaki where she could book her passage.

Clutching a ticket, Sarah settled in a café to while away the hours until boarding. It was hard to miss the white-hulled vessel painted in the blue and yellow livery of the shipping company, but the boat was smaller than the vast container ships and cruise liners coming and going from the largest port in the Eastern Mediterranean. Looking up from the book she was reading, Sarah saw the long queue of cars, lorries and motorbikes begin to move as they were waved onto the transport deck. She took this as her cue and, crossing the dockyard, boarded the vessel and was directed to the upper decks by a white-uniformed officer.

Standing at the rail, she watched as the crew cast off the giant hawsers and winched them aboard, the bows of the ship edging towards the harbour entrance and the open sea. The blue and white ensign of Greece at the stern strained on its staff as the ship made its way through the slightest of swells. Sarah was on her way to Crete.

Chapter 6

THE MOONLESS NIGHT heightened the sound of every step John took as he headed for the sea. It was as Vassilis had described, a shingle beach with rocks strewn across the gaping dried out mouth of a river that created the gorge that had become his friend's last resting place. He ducked behind a rock and waited.

The darkness and silence played with his imagination. Had he counted right, had the tender been and gone? The wait seemed as interminable as the pitch black he stared into hoping for any sign of his rescuers. If they didn't come, Vassilis had given his life in vain and the young commando was stranded and vulnerable. He thought of searching for any other soldiers attempting to make the rendezvous, but his training told him to stay put until he got a signal.

The tender was close inshore when he saw the flashing light. A short whistle came in response from behind the bluff of rock opposite where John was concealed. Adjusting his eyes, he could see nothing, but heard the gentle pull of oars on water under the whispered directions of the helmsman. The first John saw of his rescuers was the bowman, and a splash as he jumped down into the water and edged the boat ashore. John broke cover and as he did, five other men emerged from the rocks around the beach. Getting closer, he saw two men dressed in shepherd's clothing disembark the boat, speaking Greek with a heavily armed man who had approached the vessel with two of his charges.

'Welcome aboard sir.' One of the seamen smiled as John handed up the case holding the lyra before being helped up over the gunwale of the large rowing boat. As four other men were assisted onto the gig, the two shepherds disappeared into the night, following the Greek andarte.

The bowman pushed the prow of the vessel off the shingle and hauled himself aboard. Four oarsmen back-paddled away from the beach before the officer at the helm swung the tiller over and they struck out into the darkness. The men sat in silence as the crew at the oars bent to their task, pulling further away from the island. John felt a sense of regret at leaving behind a place and a people who had looked after him so well and that he had grown to love and that the man who had made his escape possible had died. He looked down at his feet and lifted the case his dead friend had given him away from the water that trickled across the bottom boards, and hugged it to his chest.

How far the men rowed was hard to judge. The thoughts John was left alone with as they eased into the heart of that darkness were as black as the void of the Libyan Sea. Astern, the shapes of the White Mountains shrank in the distance, a shadowy reminder of all that he had been through.

His thoughts were interrupted as the hull of a ship loomed above them. The size of the boat took John by surprise. When Vassilis had said the rescue boat would be a launch he had imagined something smaller. This vessel must have been more than a hundred feet in length, and climbing up the boarding ladder it took all his strength to reach the deck.

The tender winched up on davits, the thud of the engines increased to a clamour as the ship made full speed for the African coast. Ushered below decks, despite the spartan functionality of the Royal Navy vessel, John was amazed at the comfort the launch offered. Taken to a small officer's mess he was served a meal of soup, eggs, bacon, potatoes, corned beef and cheese, and a bottle of wine was opened with which to toast the king.

Travelling at 20 knots, the captain hoped to put some 130 miles between themselves and Crete before daylight, minimising the risk of attack from the air. If luck were with them, they would arrive in Egypt the following evening. Much of the time John slept, waking only to eat and drink as the motor launch sped its way across the southern Mediterranean. His sleep was dreamless; each time he awoke, it took a moment to realise where he was. With a full stomach and the rolling comfort of his bunk, the mountains of Crete already seemed far away. Then he would remember the ultimate sacrifice his friend had made to deliver him to safety and a shard of guilt punctured his wellbeing.

Standing at the rail, John could make out the smell of land before he saw it. Night had fallen as the ship felt its way through the darkened defences of the ancient harbour, a haven for warships since the times of Alexander the Great. In the blackout he could just make out the shapes of ships lying at anchor off great jetties where supply vessels unloaded military vehicles, armaments and other cargo to the dockside. How different John felt now to when he departed this port for Crete little less than a year before. The launch eased its way alongside a quay, hawsers creaking and straining every sinew as it was winched landwards. The gangplank lowered, John stepped onto African soil to be met by a uniformed driver who escorted him to a staff car for the night drive to Cairo.

The early morning streets of the capital were alive with taxis, cars and horse-drawn gharries. Parking outside a smart hotel, the driver carried John's rucksack and lyra to a room on the first floor.

'I've orders to pick you up at ten in the morning if that's OK with you, sir? I'm to drive you to headquarters for a debrief. Have a good night.' The driver saluted and left John alone.

Exhausted, he flung open the windows and shutters which opened to a small balcony, staring in amazement at the street below. Cairo seemed a million miles further away from Crete than the day's journey he had just travelled. Late-night revellers were still noisily walking the pavements and traffic hooted its way through the streets. The scene appeared more reminiscent of peacetime London than a city less than two hundred miles away from the front line in a furious theatre of war.

A uniform and some clean clothes hung in the wardrobe and despite the late hour, he ran a bath and soaked until he fell asleep enjoying that almost forgotten luxury. Drying himself, John resumed his slumbers on the bed, before the light and noise from the street below forced their way into his torpor through the open windows. Dressing in his new uniform John had time for a breakfast better than he had eaten since the war had started. He sat amongst other service officers and businessmen in the opulent surroundings of the dining room as they started their day with plates of eggs and bacon, cold meats, cheeses and fruit.

Out on the city streets, shops selling any number of luxury goods were already buzzing with customers. The peaked caps and berets of soldiers, airmen and sailors mingled among suited businessmen wearing tarboosh or fez and the occasional veiled woman, as John's driver navigated his way through the hustle and bustle to the grand building that housed Middle East Command.

In a tiny office, John learned that his commando group had already been disbanded. Less than a quarter of the force sent to Crete had made it back to Egypt. He was to be reassigned and had been billeted in a house shared with other officers to rehabilitate after his ordeal and await orders about his future.

Cairo was a revelation. It was unlike anywhere John had ever known. Coming from a provincial, rural background, he had only been to London occasionally prior to the war. Before his deployment to north Africa and Crete, he had spent some days there, but by that time the capital city was in the grip of the Blitz and already suffering the privations of rationing.

A mixture of troops on leave and support staff freed from the constraints of austerity back home had turned Cairo into a party town like no other. At first, John felt guilty about drinking from this cup of plenty when he knew how the people of Crete and his mother and father back home were suffering.

Stepping outside the social circle of Allied officers, wealthy Egyptians and expatriates, John also sensed unease at the British presence in the country. The ostentatious wealth in the heart of the city sat uncomfortably with the poverty a short stroll away along its stifling streets.

Billeted in the centre of the city close to the banks of the Nile, his housemates were two captains serving in the 7th Armoured Division, a major in the Special Forces and a press attaché at the nearby British Embassy. They were good company and wildly embraced all the city had to offer. Slowly John let down his guard. He relaxed his natural reserve and despite his initial diffidence began to enjoy Cairo, knowing his stay there would be brief.

His friends appeared to know everyone returning on leave or working for the war effort at staff headquarters, the embassy or in hospitals. The house was a meeting place where people would often gather before heading out to dine or party the night away.

Shortly after his arrival, John made the acquaintance of a Desert Rat called Douglas Harper. A tall, smiling man whose stature and personality quietly dominated any room he entered, it was the violin he carried that caught John's eye. He had not held a fiddle since the wedding in Samaria Gorge. His eagerness to pick up the instrument overcame his shyness, and John summoned the courage to ask Douglas if he could play.

It was as if he had never stopped playing. Bowing a mix of folk music and popular classics from memory, he became suffused with the emotion remembering the last time he had performed alongside Vassilis in Crete. The applause that rippled around the living room shook him from his melancholy. Douglas was keen to tell him about their group of musicians who would play at whatever

115

parties they were invited to. The line up changed from day to day as members came and went and the friendly Desert Rat asked John to join them.

'I'm afraid I don't have a violin with me, but I could maybe play the lyra?'

From his face, John could tell this meant nothing to Douglas. Going to his room, he returned clasping the talismanic instrument. Telling how he had come by it and how the catch on the case had saved his life, he took up the instrument and played the haunting melodies Vassilis had taught him. The power of the emotion in the music transported him back to the mountains of Crete, as the room fell silent under its spell. It was the first time anyone in the room had heard anything like it.

Music became the glue that held the two men together. Their shared love of playing became the foundation on which Douglas and John's comfortable rapport was founded. Over a drink, the two men would talk late into the night about their interest. Being able to perform helped John come to terms with the death of Vassilis. His music found him in demand and he formed friendships and had passing relationships with women who were drawn to the talented officer. But it was with Douglas that he made a firm bond. When his friend was recalled to the front he missed the time they had spent talking and playing music together.

The tide was turning in the desert war. Cairo celebrated to the full news of victory at El Alamein and the hounding of the Afrika Korps out of Egypt and John was asked to perform at gatherings across the city. In December, his rehabilitation considered complete, his reassignment to another Special Services group came through and John was ordered east to the Canal Zone for training.

Victories for the Allies in North Africa and news that the invasion of the Soviet Union was severely stretching German resources marked a change in fortunes in the War and attention began to focus on plans for retaking Europe. John returned home by ship on the long journey through the Suez Canal around the Horn of Africa and the Cape of Good Hope. After the heat of north Africa, the sodden highlands of Scotland proved a welcome change. Preparations were in full swing for the invasion of Europe.

His comrades were a maverick group but the one thing most had in common was their upbringing, which was a world away from John's humble beginnings. If they had any misgivings about the scholarship boy, the bravery he showed in training along with his survival in Crete and his musical prowess impressed them. Few balked at his promotion to the rank of major and privately those chosen to serve with him were relieved.

For months the men trained, jumping out of aeroplanes and parachuting into the inhospitable wilds of the hills, hiding out and living off their wits. They learned about explosives, how to kill in close contact and the art of sabotage. Although detailed plans were kept under wraps, it was an open secret that the commandoes would be deployed in the days before the invasion of Europe to divert enemy resources from the beach landings, disrupt supply chains and link up with the Resistance fighters of the Free French. Operations would be fraught with danger and not one of the soldiers was under any illusions that their life was not on the line, but to a man they were eager to do anything they could to see an end to the war.

The night before Operation Overlord John and two men under his command dropped by parachute at night to the west of Chateauroux in the Val de Loire region of central France. On a major railway line, the Germans used the town as a hub for the transport of soldiers and supplies. Far enough from the beachheads, it was hoped the raid would provide an effective diversion.

Success in sabotage operations by the Free French in the region had led to violent reprisals by the Germans that had weakened the integrity of the Resistance in the area. John and his men were to rendezvous with still extant fighters and, providing them with detonators and explosives, help cause maximum damage to the railway line.

The pilot did a good job and the lack of wind aided the accuracy of their drop. The soldiers landed within 50 yards of the flare set to guide them down. Two Resistance fighters welcomed them in hushed tones, hiding their parachutes in the nearby undergrowth before they set out to walk the two and a half miles to the target.

Progress to the railway was slower than John would have liked. In a hamlet a mile away from their target they spotted two German military motorbikes and had to take a long detour to ensure they were not spotted. The delay meant the train they planned to blow up was now only a matter of minutes away and German efficiency, even in wartime, meant they were unlikely to be bought any time.

Working with the two Frenchmen, one commando lay the charge before making the signal to retreat. A burst of gunfire rang out, obliterating the low rumble of the approaching locomotive. John saw the other commando drop. Instinct made him hit the ground. The approaching roar told John the train would be on them within the minute. Time was running out. Shouting at the men to get to a safe distance and detonate, he would cover their action. John knew he was risking his life, from where he was, the explosion would surely kill him, but advancing towards his enemy, he had a slim chance. The Germans were concentrating on the men at the rail track. John rose to his feet firing at a run. One man fell before John felt the shot hit him. Swinging his gun, he fired at a shadow in the darkness as the locomotive behind him exploded. Knocked off his feet, the adrenaline drained from his body as the agony of the injury took hold. As the dust settled, he could hear cries coming from the back of the train as enemy soldiers struggled to extricate themselves from derailed coaches. His surviving comrade and the two Resistance fighters were at his side in no time.

'He's dead, let's get you out of here, sir.' The other commando answered John's unspoken question about his fallen comrade.

Supported by his brother in arms, he was half carried back across the fields. Under the cover of a copse of trees, his fellow saboteurs applied a tourniquet to the top of his wounded arm. They were convinced their plans had been compromised and considered it too dangerous to go to the safe house. They needed to head northwest, pray the D-Day invasion succeeded and that the Allied troops would make good speed through France.

The going was slow. The cloud provided them with some cover but, where it broke, a full moon left them dangerously exposed. After three hours, they had made just two miles. When dawn came, the Resistance fighters found the two soldiers temporary refuge in a wooded area, while they went to contact members of the network to find medical assistance and a new safe house.

Exhausted and badly in need of treatment, John knew the tourniquet, although stemming the blood loss, would cause what was left of his arm to atrophy. The bullet had punctured his upper arm, shattering the humerus. John felt that at sometime he must run out of the agony he felt, but the pain was relentless. The Frenchmen returned with a doctor but bad news about finding a safe place to hide. German troops were pouring into the region on their way to the front line in an attempt to stem the tide of the invasion. Stitching the wound and applying a dressing, the doctor did what he could, but John was desperate for more medical help. The news was that the Normandy landings had been successful, although progress inland was slower than hoped. It was clear it would take weeks before any friendly forces would reach them.

They came up with a daring alternative plan, to transport the commandos in a relay of vehicles in the direction of the invading Allied army, travelling by night, hoping the retreating Germans would be too preoccupied to track the saboteurs.

Over the following days, John drifted in and out of consciousness as he was carried between vans, cars and trucks making covert night-time progress through the French countryside. Their strategy proved better than they could have imagined. They made good headway, unhindered by the Germans.

Intermittent gunfire warned they were approaching the retreating enemy's lines. It was the end of the third night and John was in desperate need of medical attention. To try to break through the rear of the enemy lines was a risk too far. The men took the decision to hole up and hope the tide of the retreat would wash over them.

Passing through a village in darkness, they were now no more than a couple of miles from gunfire. The silhouette of a huddle of farm buildings lay on the outskirts. The village itself might prove tempting cover for the retreating soldiers, so they opted to take their chances at the remote farm that they hoped the Germans would sweep straight past.

A barn offered an ideal place to hide the van and a hayloft provided the best available refuge. Through gaps in the boarded wall the uninjured men kept watch. As dawn broke, so did barrage after barrage of gunfire as Allied artillery found its range to soften up the enemy and cover the advancing tanks and light infantry. The men just had to pray their hideout would not become a target. Within two hours of the guns signalling the start of the skirmish, the German troops came into sight. The men had made the right call. The enemy retreated along the road not bothering to turn off up off the track towards the farm, heading for the cover of the village beyond.

Little more than twenty minutes after the last of the enemy army had sped past, two tanks pulled into the yard. Announcing himself in English, the commando made their presence known to his comrades. An ambulance was called to the front line, and took John to a field hospital established behind the vanguard of the advancing army.

It didn't take long for the medics to determine there was little they could do to save the arm. Within an hour of his arrival, the young major was in the makeshift operating theatre. When he came round from the anaesthetic, despite ongoing pain, he felt some relief from the agony he had been suffering. As he lay there, however, another acute trauma lodged itself in his brain: the life-changing realisation that he would never play the violin again.

In his waking moments, he could not shrug off the depression that this knowledge brought. Those flashes of lucidity became less and less as his temperature rose and he tossed and turned, mumbling in a burning sweat on the damp recovery bed. The infection that had taken hold lasted three days as doctors and nurses struggled with antibiotics, intravenous fluids and cold compresses to control the disease that was ravaging John's body.

On the fourth day, the delirium subsided. For the first time since the fever had struck, he was able to take some soup and slowly his body began to recover. As John lay alone in the hospital, the anguish struck him even more deeply at the loss of purpose he now felt.

All John was left with during those days was a dark blanket of depression, which shrouded the whole of his future. His only ambition had been to be a musician, and now that had been taken from him. The occasional attentions of a nurse or the doctors' ward rounds proved a relief from his dark thoughts, anything that could divert his mind, however briefly, from the heavy weight of solitude.

Weeks after the operation, John did not know how many, the dark cloud which encircled his head was parted by the sound of a voice he recognised. Too weak to call out his friend's name, he had to wait until a nurse came to change his dressing before he could ask if Douglas Harper was a patient in the hospital. She promised to find out and was as good as her word. Within half an hour the tall gunner officer was standing over John's bed.

'I'd have recognised that voice anywhere,' opened John. 'It's so good to see a familiar face.'

Seeing his friend's smile let a chink of light into the blackness of John's soul.

'Fancy bumping into you here,' replied Douglas lightly, disguising the distress he felt at his friend's condition. 'You look pretty shot up.'

The two men discussed what had brought them there and the extent of their injuries. Douglas immediately dismissed the bullet he had taken through the hand as the graze from a sniper's round that had hit when he'd been observing from the cupola of his tank. He could tell whatever light John tried to make of his horrific injury he was in a dark place. The glint had gone from his eyes and staring into them was like peering into an abyss.

Knowing his friend's passion, Douglas was aware how hard it would be for John to lose his arm. He tried to avoid the subject but it was clear that what had brought them together in Cairo had been their love of music. It seemed that all the common ground they shared was rooted in that mutual infatuation.

Instead of avoiding the subject, Douglas became aware that talking about their memories of Egypt and confronting the consequences of John's injury began to have a positive effect on his friend. It was early days, but through their companionship John began to see there might be a future without playing the violin, he just needed to find it. Douglas was a good listener. He gave John the space to talk. He knew his friend's strength of character from his exploits in Crete, but was aware that coming to terms with his injuries would take time.

As the days and weeks went by the war was moving further and further away from them, as the Allied advance moved eastwards. The two friends were to be moved in the opposite direction and transferred to England for rehabilitation. An ambulance carrying the casualties made its way through the French countryside against the tide of troops and supplies flooding towards the front line.

When the injured servicemen reached the port of Cherbourg, the devastation all around them was apparent. Swathes of the city had been obliterated. Following its liberation by American troops,

125

no time had been wasted in sweeping for mines and opening up the sea lanes. The quays were repaired and new cranes erected as engineers and troops laboured to create what was to become, for a time, the busiest port in the world.

With John in a ward in the bowels of a Royal Navy hospital ship, Douglas stood on deck watching the coast of France fade into the distance. As the boat laboured against a grey swell towards Portsmouth, Douglas knew that for him it was likely to be a short respite from action but for his friend it was obvious that his war was over.

They sailed past the Isle of Wight into the Solent and cruised nearby the sea forts protecting the entrance to Portsmouth harbour, where ships stood at anchor. The berths at the quaysides were a hive of activity as supplies were loaded bound for France. John and Douglas' progress was to prove more sedate as an ambulance trundled them through the dockyard gates into the Hampshire and Surrey countryside. They swept up the drive of the hospital, a building that clearly had in happier times, been very grand. Requisitioned as a hospital it still provided a level of comfort unimaginable in the field hospital. There were gardens through which patients could walk or be pushed on paths around lawns and shaded glades, and doctors and nurses had more time to attend to the wider needs of their patients. The two friends had requested that they be placed in the same ward, and as time went on John felt able to be wheeled by Douglas through the hospital grounds.

The leaves on the trees turned golden and an edge on the breeze heralded the end of summer. The last blooms had begun to wilt by the time John discarded his wheelchair and felt strong enough to walk again. He was pleased when the nurse assigned to accompany him as he found his feet was the small, slender, dark-haired young woman who had sometimes attended him on the ward. Her gentle movements as she walked across the polished floors matched her soft, friendly voice and he felt comfortable in her presence. It seemed as though she had all the time in the world as he adjusted to taking those first tentative steps outside.

Although the physical scars were healing, it was clear to Douglas that confronting the demons born out of his injury would prove a tougher battle for the young commando. He recognised the mental effort his friend was asserting to try and wrench his thoughts from all negativity about his uncertain future.

John's parents came to visit. He was looking forward to some company that did not remind him of the army and the war. As they entered the ward, he glimpsed their pain and they looked older than he remembered. In the second before they readjusted their expressions to a mask of smiles, John could sense their anguish. Despite his parents' best intentions, their presence made John even more aware of the impact of his wounds.

Although impressed by the tall, softly spoken artillery officer, it was his badly injured friend towards whom Marion Blunt felt drawn. She had joined up with the Queen Alexandra's Royal Army Nursing Corps two years earlier and after training had been posted to the Surrey hospital specialising in the rehabilitation of servicemen. Although she had found training easy, dealing with so many badly injured troops had proved a challenging journey for the sensitive young woman. Her empathy served her well and although it took an emotional toll, the attractive nurse's bedside manner had made her popular with the men for whom she cared.

Behind her gentle manner there lay a determination in Marion to make a difference to the lives of others. That steely core had proved of great value when this girl with a sheltered upbringing had been forced to confront the horrors of war, but from deep inside she found the resolve to put such feelings to the back of her mind and do all she could to make those in her care more comfortable.

From the easy talking Desert Rat, Marion learned the little he knew about John's past and of his broken dream. The more Douglas spoke of his friend's bravery in Crete and France the more she felt attracted to John. There was something beneath the glazed surface of his eyes that burned brighter. Beyond his closed exterior, she sensed a depth of sincerity and creativity she was keen to explore. Although the other officers she treated were kind, with most she keenly felt the gaping gulf in social class between her own humble background and theirs. She was comfortable with the modest young commando who never spoke about his achievements. Self-effacing about his acts of bravery and stoic in the face of all he had lost, John's kind demeanour exerted a powerful pull over Marion who saw beyond the injuries of the young major. As he grew stronger, the nurse sought every opportunity to walk with John in the gardens of the hospital. As the days went on the friendship that had grown between them blossomed into an attraction that soon developed into love.

Douglas knew it wouldn't be long, and several months after arriving back in England, notice of his recall to France came through. If the news upset John, he tried not to show it.

'Keep your head down this time, I don't want to see you back here,' were the words the major with an empty jacket sleeve pinned to his side used to cover the welter of emotions he felt as his friend walked out of the hospital doors. Looking back, Douglas saw Marion wrap an arm around John's shoulders as they turned and walked back inside.

Chapter 7

SLEEP HAD WORKED wonders on Sarah's mood as she stepped out of the hotel in Heraklion. Tempted by the brightly lit cafes on Lion Square she decided the bustle of the evening crowd would distract her from the plans she needed to make, and determined to go wherever the streets might take her.

Walking the narrow byways of the town, stepping aside to avoid the scooters and cars that drove at improbable speeds in all directions, she found a taverna on the corner where the lanes met the coast road. At a table precariously balanced on the narrow pavement outside, she took a seat.

A waiter appeared, with a flourish clipping a white paper cloth to the table. He invited her into the kitchen to view the dishes on offer: fish on a bed of ice in a glass cabinet; a fridge full of pork chops, cuts of lamb and skewers of souvlaki; and a hot plate with trays of chicken, roasted potatoes, meatballs, stuffed peppers and spaghetti.

'The fish is fresh today. I buy it myself from a boat in the harbour. I have red mullet, sea bream, small fishes and octopus.'

Pointing out a sea bream, Sarah then ordered a small carafe of white. After the first taste of the steely chilled wine, her palate adjusted to its refreshing dryness. Reaching into her bag, she unearthed the map Yannis had marked out back in England.

Most of the blue rings circled locations a long way to the west. These included the few places she knew her grandfather had passed through during the war. She recognised some of the names ringed to the east, Spinalonga, Vai, Lassithi Plateau... but they would take her in the opposite direction. Having read about the island being the site of the first European civilisation she was determined not to leave Heraklion without having visited the nearby Minoan palace of Knossos.

The bream was simply grilled, its skin crisp and salty, tasting of the sea which lay a stone's throw away, served with lemon sauce, potatoes fried in olive oil and a salad topped with olives and creamy feta cheese. Along with a second carafe of wine, it was the perfect accompaniment to the making of plans. As she sat replete, the waiter brought her a plate of fresh fruit and a small carafe of clear liquid and two glasses.

'You like raki?' The taverna quiet, he gestured his request to sit at the table.

'I've never tasted it before,' replied Sarah, wondering if it was wise to drink more.

He poured a measure into each of the two glasses and holding up his, toasted Sarah. '*Yamas!* To our health!' The waiter clinked his glass on hers.

The sharpness of the spirit made Sarah wince, but she liked the taste.

'*Yamas*,' echoed Sarah. 'And thank you for a great meal.'

'*Parakalo*, you are welcome, where are you travelling to?'

'I think I should go to Knossos tomorrow, then I will head west.'

'You should go early to Knossos. Many people arrive by coach and it gets very crowded,' advised the waiter.

He was amazed when Sarah announced she would go on foot. Looking on the map she estimated the walk was about four miles and an early morning stroll would allow her to see more of the city and the surrounding countryside. With the knowledge that the site opened at eight o'clock, she determined to set off at dawn. Paying the bill Sarah stood to leave.

'*Kalispera. Efharisto*. Good evening. Thank You.'

'*Efharisto*,' repeated Sarah as she turned to head back to the hotel.

The sun had not yet risen as Sarah left her hotel. From its hiding place somewhere to the east, the first signals of its intent began to filter into the sky, diluting the darkness. It was Sunday; the owners of cafés in Lion Square sleepily opened shutters whilst some early risers sipped coffee and water and twirled their *komboloi* worry beads. In contrast to the mayhem of the previous day on the market the stalls remained covered and the shops closed.

Reaching the Bembo Fountain on Plateia Kornarou she joined Evans Street, following it through the city walls to meet the dusty Leoforos Knossou. As the sun rose, the clamour of the Sunday church bells rang to wake the sleeping metropolis. The sun began to find its strength and she was grateful for her early start.

Idle cranes rose from boarded up building sites, marking the border of the ever-expanding city as it sprawled further into the hillside surrounding the capital. There was little countryside left between the suburbs and the new settlement of souvenir shops and tavernas that had sprung up around the ancient palace.

Stepping on to the site of the palace it was clear to Sarah that the walk had been worth it. Reading the guidebook she bought at the entrance she learned that the standing columns and deeply coloured frescoes were reconstructions, built by the British archaeologist Arthur Evans and his team at the beginning of the twentieth century. It was Evans who had named the palace and the civilisation that built it as Minoan.

However authentic or otherwise the work might be, it helped Sarah imagine that first European civilisation. Drawn by three red pillars framing a fresco of a bull, on turning round the whole palace lay before her, the remains of more than a thousand interconnecting rooms surrounding a square.

This 'new palace' dated from between 1700 to 1450 BCE, she read. The original building that occupied the site was built two hundred years previously, and destroyed by an earthquake. Evidence suggests there were settlements in the area going back a further seven hundred years...

Sarah sat in the shade of a column to read more. So much of the Cretan culture was bound up in this spot where, she read, the son of Zeus, King Minos, kept hidden the Minotaur, the half man, half beast offspring of his wife and a bull.

Legend had it that, in his shame, the king imprisoned the bull in a labyrinth designed by Daedalus, feeding it a diet of young men and virgins shipped in from Athens until Theseus, with the help of Minos' daughter Ariadne, slew the beast. So many myths that Sarah recalled from her schooldays seemed linked to the maze of buildings and alleyways that lay before her. The streets of the palace could be taken for the labyrinth.

Whatever the truth about the legends, Sarah was happy to suspend disbelief. She explored the streets where staircases connected different levels of higgledy-piggledy buildings that had been served with under-floor heating, flushing toilets, water and sewage pipes some three and a half thousand years before cities like London benefitted from such luxuries.

A fresco indicating a link between the mythical Minotaur and Minoan society along with murals of priestesses and flying dolphins adorned the palace walls. The scale of the ruins was colossal, and the awe-inspiring images transported her back in time.

The wonders of the palace in her mind as she walked back to Heraklion, Sarah began to understand why Yannis had been so passionate about the island of his birth. She felt closer to the essence of Crete, to its spirit, and more determined to unravel the part the island had played in her grandfather's past.

Back at the hotel, she took the lyra from the case and began to play. The music Yannis had taught her came easily, as though the lyra felt a sense of familiarity in its surroundings knowing it had returned home at last.

The following day's trip from Heraklion to Chania would take nearly three hours. Sarah had so little information to go on. From what the regimental archivist had told her, John had landed on a beach at Souda Bay near Chania, so it seemed a good place to start her journey of discovery. Following the coast road out of the city, the bus joined the national highway winding its way into the mountains. She caught enticing glimpses of the sea before the road darted inland. Signposts indicated the precarious way down to tiny seaside villages and Sarah recognised the name of Agia Pelagia, the resort Liz had visited with her hapless boyfriend.

The further from Heraklion the bus travelled, the more rugged the landscape became. Olive groves clung to slopes topped with lonely whitewashed chapels and in the distance mountain peaks stood majestic, their crowns still glistening with the last snows of winter.

On arrival in Chania finding a room was easy. Booking in, Sarah deposited her luggage. She walked to the old Venetian port, strolling along the long defensive sea wall to the lighthouse that stood sentinel at its entrance, before turning to look at the effortlessly sublime city stretching inland. Taking a seat at one of the waterside cafés, she ate a late breakfast before setting out to find a taxi for Souda Bay.

'I'll take you there miss, but where exactly do you want to go?' the driver asked. 'It's a big bay – the airport, the naval base, the war cemetery or somewhere else?'

'I'm not sure.' Sarah explained to the driver that she wanted to see where her grandfather had landed on Crete all those years ago, but the landing of Layforce meant nothing to him.

'Perhaps I drop you at the graveyard,' he offered.

With no better suggestion, Sarah accepted. They drove along the road towards the small settlement of Souda, among groves of olive and eucalyptus trees until the taxi drew up outside the Allied War Cemetery.

Pots of plants flanked the iron gates inscribed on either side 1939 and 1945 that opened onto a well-watered lawn surrounding an imposing white stone cross. Both left and right of the memorial an avenue had been created by row upon row of the pristine headstones in memory of 1,500 Allied servicemen, many in unnamed graves, who had lost their lives fighting to keep Crete free. As Sarah passed through the gates, she was moved to tears by the scale of the loss and the beautiful poignancy of this cemetery that ran down to the sea.

The faint clipping of a lone gardener tending the graves was all that broke the silence. Looking out across the serene waters of the bay it was hard to imagine what it must have been like as battle raged here some seventy years before.

'You look lost, can I help you?' Sarah's reverie was broken by the gardener. 'I know where each of the named fallen are buried. It is sad that for so many of the graves we don't know who they are.'

'I was just thinking how beautiful and peaceful it is here,' answered Sarah. 'I haven't come to find a grave, just to try and find out more about my granddad who fought here.'

'I'll help if I can,' smiled the gardener. 'Tell me what you know about your grandfather's story.'

137

Walking between the rows of memorial stones, the gardener and Sarah then sat looking seawards. As a ferry made its way across the Sound, past the ancient fortified island of Nea Souda and out to sea, Sarah told her story to the caretaker who spent his life attending the graves of the victims of the conflict.

As her grandfather was part of a covert group, he believed the exact spot that he landed was unknown, although she could follow his footsteps through Imbros Gorge to Chora Sfakion and, also, down Tripitis Gorge to the beach where he was rescued. Like Yannis, he believed that the most likely place for him to have hidden out was around the gorge of Samaria but he could be no more specific.

Realising it was unlikely she would learn more, Sarah was unsure where knowing any more particularities about her grandfather's time on Crete would take her. Surely, it was her love for the lyra that had led her here? It was to get to the core of Crete so she could play with the passion of a Cretan and through that journey resolve a way to move on with her life. Her grandfather had always steered her course with the lightest of hands on the tiller. In that moment by the beach in Souda, Sarah knew he was still guiding her.

Chora Sfakion would be a good base from which to explore the south west, advised the gardener. From there she could board boats to travel the coast or catch buses to the heads of the gorges.

The point of departure for so many soldiers escaping the island became her starting point. Where it would lead her, Sarah decided to leave to serendipity.

The bus journey from Chania to Chora Sfakion was spectacular and at times nerve-wracking as the coach switchbacked its way through the White Mountains, rising to the Plateau of Askifou. Surrounded by the towering peaks of Kastro in the west, Agathes to the south and Tripali to the east, they crossed a tapestry of cultivated fields before plunging downwards round the hairpin bends that somehow threaded the road between the gorges of Imbros and Sfakiano to the sea.

Finding a room above a taverna on the seafront, she walked the path following the coast, past the memorial to the evacuation. The flag of Greece fluttered alongside those of Britain, Australia and New Zealand above a plaque telling the story of the battle. An engraving of two exhausted soldiers wading out to an awaiting boat stood next to a single canon pointing out to sea. It was here that her grandfather had learned that there would be no more ships coming to take him to safety and thousands of troops had settled down to await capture.

After a dinner of chunks of smoked pork and potatoes baked in herbs, oil and lemon followed by cheese pastries drizzled with honey, as the sun set over the White Mountains Sarah made plans to descend through the Imbros Gorge the following day.

Awoken by the wind beating on the unsecured shutters and waves pounding the beach below her apartment balcony, Sarah lay in the dark, thoughts swirling. At last, tiredness took her again. She eventually came round to the sound of chairs and tables being arranged in the taverna below. She opened the shutters to a sky washed clear blue by the rain. The sea had resumed its calm demeanour, the only vestiges of the storm a mere ripple sucking and blowing at the sands beneath her balcony.

To get to the top of the gorge, she took the bus that made its way into the foothills of the mountains, retracing some of the journey of the previous day. She smiled to herself as the driver turned on the radio. Lyra music played an accompaniment as he swung his vehicle around the tight bends. Behind her, the Libyan Sea stretched out like a swatch of periwinkle silk in the early morning haze. She was keen to get started on the walk but happy as the bus slowed to follow a goatherd, a crook resting on his shoulders, his dogs guiding the flock along the road to pastures new.

From 2,500 feet above the sea, the gorge dropped for five miles to the coast to the east of Chora Sfakion. Sitting on a rock at the head of the gorge, she changed into walking boots, exchanging them in her pack with the trainers she had been wearing. Setting off, trees of fig and almond flourished among the ever-present cypresses as the path narrowed and the walls gained height closing

140

in on the uneven stones that marked the route taken by that bedraggled army of 12,000 soldiers in 1941. To Sarah the walk was benign enough, but she imagined how, crowded with defeated, frightened, hungry men threatened by ambush and the constant attention of enemy planes the trek must have been a nightmare. As the sides of the gorge closed in, a chill ran through her. Caves pockmarked the grizzled visage of the rocks mottled white, grey and golden as the light pierced through the shadows of the trees impossibly high above.

Where earlier Sarah had felt free, claustrophobia descended as the walls pressed in on her and she could reach out and touch both sides of the canyon. Unable to shake thoughts of those dark days of war, it was with relief that she sensed the light change, revealing she was getting closer to the sea – as if an invisible Ariadne's thread was leading her from the labyrinth.

An hour's walk beside the calming sea back to Chora Sfakion went some way to restoring Sarah's composure but her face told a different story as she took a seat at the taverna beneath her room. With a cold beer came concern from the owner.

'Why you look so sad in the most beautiful place on earth?'

Sarah felt surprised that her face had betrayed the emotions, which for some time had been churning inside her.

The owner followed the beer with *mezzes* and raki and as he sat with Sarah her mood lifted. 'Tomorrow you should go to

141

Loutro. No buses, no cars, no worries. It will make you happy,' he advised. 'You stay one, two days or more and come back a new person.' He offered to look after her things until her return, whenever that might be

A few essentials in her holdall, the next morning Sarah boarded the ferry for the short trip along the coast. Sitting on the starboard side of the ferry *Neptune*, Sarah watched as the vessel slipped past the cliffs where the White Mountains topple into the sea, then coasted beside an isolated beach where a line of stunted trees grew out of the pebbles. A lone chapel perched on the mountainside, the sole mark of man visible until Loutro revealed itself. Clinging to the stark mountains, the glinting village looked out upon the sparkling blue waters from which the ferry approached.

Neptune turned inshore of a small island, its lighthouse guarding the western approaches to the crescent-shaped bay as a few fishing boats and a caique bobbed on their moorings in its wake. On disembarking, the ferry headed once more to sea. As the regular beat of its engines faded, the silence was palpable.

Walking the narrow alleys of the village, Sarah found a pension before settling down to a breakfast of yoghurt, fruit and honey in a waterside taverna. Then she went down to lie on the beach, and Loutro began to work its magic. It was hard not to agree that this was a perfect place to restore her wellbeing.

142

Sarah was one of just a few early season visitors to the village. Although still spring, the sun was hot. Even though the sea was cold she held her breath and dived in. When she was not reading or sleeping, she strolled to the taverna for cold drinks. Returning to her room a late siesta turned into a full-blown sleep and by the time she awoke the sun was already low. She emerged just in time to see the golden orb suffuse the sky with a wash of red, illuminating the mountains in an orange glow before receding in purple shadow.

The last ferry had departed, the village left to the locals and few outsiders staying over. Feeling the pull of familiarity, Sarah returned to the taverna where she had breakfast. Hungry, she ordered a plate brimming with mixed fish; calamari, whitebait, sardines, prawns and sea bass. The ripple of the sea washing the sand was the only accompaniment to her meal. Sitting at a table in the open air beside the sea her thoughts turned to her granddad, and she welled up with the gratitude she felt towards him for leading her there. Not once did Gareth cross her mind. She reached in her bag for her phone and sent texts to Liz and Yannis. Then a familiar sound wrested her from her thoughts.

A lyra, guitar and laouto were being tuned by three men inside the taverna. As soon as the bow was drawn across the lyra's strings Sarah felt goose bumps on her arms and an involuntary smile break across her face. Having now experienced for herself the magical landscape of the island, more than ever the soaring melodies of the lyra spoke to her. Peering through the window, Sarah could make out the men laughing and chatting in between playing as they sat at a table eating mezzes and drinking.

Longing to enter, her shyness held her back. Whether it was the cool of the spring night or the music coming from within, she felt herself shiver. Clearing her plate the waiter urged her to sit inside where he would bring her fruit and raki.

'*Kalispera*. Good evening,' the smiling lyra player greeted her.

'*Kalispera*', replied Sarah, heading for a small table in the corner.

'No, you come and join us, sit here please,' the musician gestured with his bow to a seat next to him.

Sarah's natural reserve told her to decline but the music and the young man's smile and glinting eyes overcame any reticence she might otherwise have felt. Was it the lure of the lyra or something else? Sarah could not tell, but she was aware of feeling unusually self-conscious under the piercing brown eyes of the tall, handsome musician who had spoken to her.

'I am Nikos. My friends are Lefteris and Georgos.'

'I'm Sarah. You play beautifully.'

Sarah's face flushed slightly as she heard herself compliment the stranger.

'Thank you, Sarah,' replied Nikos rolling her name around his mouth like a fine wine. 'Do you like the music?'

'I love the music.' Sarah's eyes dropped as Nikos' gaze met hers. When he began to play again she could not take her eyes off him as the music drew her in. With the lyra in his hand, the way Nikos became one with everything around him reminded her of Yannis, for Sarah his music became the spirit of the island she was growing to love so much.

Nikos' manner did much to make Sarah feel comfortable, but beneath her friendly smile and amiable chatter she felt a confusion of emotions she had not experienced before. She hung on Nikos' words learning that the men had been friends since their schooldays in a village near Chania. Now they worked in different places so could rarely get together. Nikos worked as a waiter in a taverna in the seaside resort of Kalyves on Souda Bay whilst Lefteris and Georgos ran a diving school in Paleochora along the coast from Loutro.

Sarah was reluctant to reveal too much of herself but as the wine and raki flowed she relaxed into the company. She realised she was drawn to Nikos and wary of the emotions she was feeling towards a man she had met barely an hour earlier. Every sign was telling her that the young Greek seemed to like her, but her limited experience of reading the signals made her untrusting of her own judgement. Even if she put aside what she could only believe was an instant attraction for Nikos, maybe he could at least help her fulfil one of the reasons she had come to the island. Could he take

145

up where Yannis had left off in teaching her the music she had fallen in love with?

'Can I see the lyra?' Sarah plucked up the courage to ask.

'Of course,' Nikos handed the instrument to her, looking in surprise as the beautiful stranger rested it on her leg and drew the bow across the strings. Lefteris and Georgos immediately fell silent as they listened in amazement to this English girl who could play the lyra.

It was as if a light had been turned on inside his head. Nikos had felt an instant attraction to the small dark-haired Englishwoman beneath whose green eyes he felt hidden depths he was keen to explore. When she played those first notes on the lyra he knew that he needed to get to know her better. What he felt was new to him; it was more than physical and went deep within him.

'*Bravo. Opa!*' Nikos encouraged, concealing the turmoil of emotions he felt inside. Overcoming their amazement, his two friends picked up their instruments and joined in with an accompaniment. The song over, Nikos held out both his arms and raised his eyebrows at once enjoining her to keep playing and enquiring how she had come to be able to play. To the encouragement of her new friends, Sarah moved through her repertoire. Nikos still could not believe what he was hearing.

Sarah knew she had some explaining to do. When she had exhausted the songs which Yannis had taught her she passed the

146

lyra back to Nikos before embarking on the story about her grandfather. As she talked, Nikos felt a growing affection for this talented, pretty girl from England whose eyes shone brightly when she played the music he so loved. She talked with such passion about her granddad and all he had done for her, about her music and the lyra the old man had left for her in a chest in an attic back in England before he died.

As Sarah told her tale, it was not like speaking to a stranger. The warmth in the deep brown eyes beneath the furrowed brow of the dark-haired musician showed he hung on every word of her story. Already she felt comfortable with this man she had just met.

It was getting late. Sarah knew if she wanted to ask Nikos if he would take her on as a pupil, she would have to take the plunge before they went their separate ways. Plucking up the courage, her face reddened.

'Would you consider having me as a student, giving me lessons on the lyra?' As soon as Sarah asked the question, she saw a shadow cast over the young man's gaze. She tried to take her request back.

'I'm sorry, I've been too forward, please, forget I asked.'

'No, it is me who should apologise, but it is impossible.' Nikos' words closed the conversation down like a door slammed in Sarah's face. The young Cretan felt ashamed at his brusque response. He felt sure his expression betrayed his disappointment at missing the chance to get closer to this beautiful, perplexing woman.

'That's fine,' an embarrassed Sarah said quickly trying to rewind the evening. But why the sadness in Nikos' face? They moved the conversation away from music and Sarah explained she wanted to visit the gorges of Samaria and Tripitis and find the beach where her grandfather had been rescued. But the magic had been sucked from the evening and Sarah stood to make her farewells.

'I could take you there. To Samaria and Tripitis I mean,' Nikos burst out, not wanting to see Sarah walk from his life. 'I am here for another six days, staying in Paleochora with my uncle, we could visit the mountains together?'

'That would be nice,' was all an elated Sarah could say, sitting back down. What remained of the evening they spent making plans. Both of them keen to grasp the chance to spend time in each other's company they tried to push aside the awkwardness of Nikos' earlier rejection.

That night Sarah lay awake in bed turning over in her head the events of the evening. Had she misread the signals she thought Nikos had given her? After all she had a history of misreading men. He seemed so enthusiastic about her playing but so adamant he would not help her to improve. What was it about this man to whom she felt an instant attraction that he would not help her to follow her dream but would give up the next few days to lead her through the White Mountains? However many times she thought about the night, she felt nothing but confusion. Perhaps she had scared him by being too forward, maybe after some time alone together he would change his mind.

Two days later, Sarah stood on the quay at Agia Roumeli awaiting the morning ferry from Paleochora. The day after the evening in the taverna, she had returned to Chora Sfakion to stuff some clean clothes in her backpack and ask the owner of the rooms if she could leave her precious luggage in his care again before taking the first ferry the next day to meet Nikos at the bottom of Samaria Gorge.

As the dot on the horizon got closer an involuntary smile spread on Sarah's face. Inside she felt excitement, tinged with nerves at meeting Nikos again. That night in Loutro she had enjoyed several drinks – would she feel the same about embarking on this journey with the personable Cretan in the cold light of day?

Sarah needn't have worried. As he stepped off the ferry, Nikos' smile banished any doubts she might have had about seeing him again. She was pleased that along with a small pack, strung across his back was the lyra. She longed to hear him play again.

Setting off across the beach they picked their way over the boulder-strewn dry bed of the river towards the bottom of the gorge. They were climbing up through the canyon and would have to find somewhere to stay on Omalos Plateau before climbing Mount Gigilos. They would then descend Tripitis Gorge to the beach where Lefteris and Georgos had agreed to pick them up in their dive boat.

A shepherd leading his flock wished them '*kalimera*' as they crossed the stream that had carved out this wonder of nature. It was not long before they reached the point where the soaring walls of the gorge were little more than Sarah's outstretched arms apart. Being there she could see how the canyon would make an ideal refuge.

They climbed upwards against a growing tide of trekkers descending the gorge, content in each other's company Sarah was captivated by the love her new friend showed for the mountains. He identified eagles and vultures hovering on thermals high above, and picked herbs from the ground for Sarah to smell. They stopped and ate a lunch of bread and cheese at the village of Samaria, which had been abandoned when the gorge became a national park in 1962.

The walk uphill was exhausting. Stopping for breath at the small church of Agios Nikolaos, Nikos excitedly pointed between the trees and Sarah glimpsed a goat with long curved horns making away into the forest of pine and eucalyptus. 'A *kri-kri*' enthused Nikos. It was native to Crete and an endangered species since hunted to near extinction for food during the deprivation of the Second World War.

Near the top of the gorge the path got tougher. When Nikos reached for her hand, Sarah did not draw back. She was grateful of his strong arm helping her up the steeper rock-strewn gradients. By the time the pair had reached the summit of their 4,000-foot climb, she was exhausted. An arm around her shoulder and the thought of a hot shower were the only things keeping Sarah going as they walked across the plateau of wild flowers, through orchards of apple blossom to the village of Omalos.

The steaming shower eased the aches in Sarah's legs but along with the dust and grime of the day's exertions washed away any trace of energy that remained. Collapsing on her bed she fell into the deepest of sleeps. Waking up, she hurried downstairs to the taverna attached to the hotel to find Nikos patiently waiting. His smile told her no apology was needed.

Looking out across the imposing shadows of the White Mountains, they shared a salad of tomatoes, onion, cucumber and feta cheese, and lamb souvlaki marinated in yoghurt and garlic and laced with peppers onions and tomatoes, served with crispy golden potatoes fried in olive oil. The meal over, they ordered another carafe of the heady dry golden wine redolent of oranges and the parched earth which engendered the extraordinary grapes from which it was made.

Sarah could hear herself gushing about all she had seen on the climb and reined herself in by reaching for her glass. Catching

Nikos' stare, his eyes met hers as though he was looking deep inside her. Reaching across the table he took her hand.

An arm draped across her as she awoke confirmed she had not been dreaming as Sarah stared lovingly at the sleeping body next to her. Her gaze roused Nikos from his sleep and he smiled as she planted a kiss on his cheek and slipped from the bed, gathered up her clothes and returned to her own room to pack her belongings in readiness for the climb of Mount Gigilos.

Chapter 8

STANDING AT THE gates of the hospital, John promised himself he would never look back. Marion had accepted his proposal of marriage and he was determined to forge a future for the both of them. He loved her deeply and felt if it had not been for her care he would have struggled to recover from his injury. The only way he could see to deal with the horrors of war was to shove them to the back of his mind. Holding his case in his one hand, the empty sleeve of his other arm pinned to his side, he knew that would take all the strength of will that he could muster.

Some months later, John's parents were proud when the medal was pinned on their son's chest. As Marion watched the emotion on her fiancé's face at the ceremony, she knew the pain she glimpsed was not for the loss of his arm but for the loss of his chosen future. And what the future held for him without music.

Back at his parents' house, John changed from his uniform, which he carefully folded. The mark of his bravery was returned to its padded case. Along with his service medals, great coat, other uniforms and the lyra, they were placed in his army chest. He clicked the lid closed and with it tried to shut away the pain of the past forever.

John did not see the chest again until five years later after he and Marion managed to scrape enough money together to buy the cottage, where it was moved to the attic along with his violin.

Marion had saved him. Through her love she had made him see there was a future. Following their wedding, with a small disability pension, Marion's wage as a nurse and a grant offered for people to train as teachers, John got a place at university, and after graduation, did his teaching certificate before taking a post at a school in Surrey.

When Marion gave birth to their son, Andrew, it seemed the couple had at last found happiness. John proved to be a good teacher who grew to love his work, helping form the young minds of a new generation.

If the young teacher and his wife had wanted another child, it was not to be and they showered Andrew with all the love they could give. The couple were devoted to each other, and through his family life and the children John taught at school, he began to rekindle optimism for the future. He became able to feel pride at the small milestones in life: Andrew starting school, going to university, getting a job, falling in love and getting married to Caroline. However, when Sarah came along, it was his granddaughter that he doted on. With Sarah, he didn't feel the massive weight of responsibility that he had felt with Andrew. They were a close family and John and Marion would spend a long time in the company of the engaging grandchild who they both loved to spoil.

When he was 65 John retired from his teaching job, every day he would meet the little girl from school before returning to the cottage for tea until her parents picked her up after work. These were the happiest times he could remember.

The stroboscopic blue light bounced off their bedroom wall and woke up John and Marion that terrible night. Insistent hammering on the door hurried John from his bed and he opened it to two policemen. Asking to come in, they broke the news of the accident. Out for an anniversary meal, the head-on collision with a driver who had lost control of his car would have killed Andrew and Caroline instantly.

How John found the strength to comfort a distraught Marion he did not know and his thoughts almost immediately turned to his little granddaughter who had lost her mum and dad. Accompanying the police to his son's house to break the news of the accident to his granddaughter and the babysitter was one of the hardest things he had faced in life. There had been no discussion; it had been such a natural thing for their beloved grandchild to come into their care. Somehow, from deep in the depths of their own grief, they managed to comfort their granddaughter.

That day Sarah moved into the cottage, it became her home and her grandparents stepped into the tragic void left in her life by the death of her mother and father. When they were with her, John and Marion were cheerful but sometimes, when they thought she was not looking, Sarah could see the distress etched on her grandparents' faces.

The first Christmas following the accident, John never knew if it had been the emotion of seeing the pictures of his son that had prompted him to confront that part of his past he had tried so hard to forget but excusing himself, he sneaked into the loft and got down his violin. Dusting off the case he wrestled with tape and Christmas paper and wrapped it as best he could.

Seeing the joy on the face of his granddaughter as she tore open the makeshift wrapping, opening the case to reveal the violin, he knew he had done the right thing. Marion smiled, knowing what the violin meant to her husband. His initial instincts were proved right when it became apparent that his grandaughter had a natural affinity for playing.

156

Over the coming years John took great pride in Sarah's achievements: playing solo at school, passing her grades, getting into the National Youth Orchestra. Even if her acceptance at the Royal College of Music had brought back a hint of regret for his own lost opportunity, it filled him with joy.

Throughout these years, Marion had shared all the highs and lows of life with the man she had nursed back to health during the war. For all that time they had been as much in love as ever. Since the death of their son, he had been her rock. Sometimes, when she was alone, she thought she would never have coped with the tragedy without him.

When John found Marion collapsed on the bathroom floor one night she was rushed by ambulance to hospital where a tumour was discovered in her stomach. The cancer had spread and within two weeks of the diagnosis Marion died.

His wife's death hit John hard. They had not been apart since the day they married. If it had not been for Sarah, his grief might have pitched him into a pit of despair. Knowing that they only had each other to lean on strengthened their relationship. In time, John's sorrow at the death of the woman he so loved became less painful to bear and he found comfort in Sarah's success; her graduation and then becoming a professional musician helped him through the grief and loneliness.

Although there had been something about Gareth he had not liked, if he had been uncertain of his granddaughter's engagement to him, he had put it to one side. If the man made Sarah happy, then he was prepared to accept him for her sake and when she had asked him to walk her down the aisle at the wedding he was overjoyed. He had died a contented man.

Chapter 9

AS DAWN BROKE over the Lefka Ori, Sarah eased her aching body into the trek. Nikos seemed to glide across the rocks as they began their ascent of Mount Gigilos. Any soreness she felt from the previous day's climb could not detract from Sarah's mood. After last night, she was sure that Nikos had feelings for her, his initial rebuffal forgotten.

If Nikos' step was light, the confusion he felt inside weighed heavily. He knew that after they left the mountains he would never see this girl again, and although usually this would not have bothered him, this time he felt something different. Perhaps if he just surrendered himself to the moment, the guilt that was taking the edge off his day would disappear and he would deal with his feelings when the time came.

Nikos thought it likely that this was the way John had hiked to get to Tripitis Gorge. The lyra swinging from Nikos' back was a reminder of when they met in Loutro, but after last night Sarah felt she now had more invested in their relationship. If she trod carefully maybe she could learn further about her new lover.

They had begun their climb near where they had left the Samaria Gorge the previous day. At the top of a winding path they looked back on the Omalos Plateau before the track flattened and descended through a rock arch to a freshwater spring. The ice-cold water was welcome as they refreshed their faces and topped up the water bottles.

Emerging above the tree line, the young Cretan wove a story of the god Zeus who had used the slopes they now climbed to preside over chariot races. The spring from which they had drunk was the site of an ancient oracle visited by those in search of wisdom and a glimpse into the future.

Nikos wondered why he had been so impulsive. Why had he agreed to bring the young Englishwoman to the mountains? When he told her he could not teach her the lyra he could have left it like that and let her walk from his life. Now, as he spent time with her, he felt his affection growing stronger by the minute. There was something about this small, fiercely independent woman, who had travelled to Crete to study the music he so loved and walk in the footsteps of her grandfather through these mountains, that attracted him deeply. It would make it all the more difficult to leave once their trek was over.

Sarah was captivated by the beauty of the mountains and enchanted by the legends that rooted them in the past. She wondered if her grandfather had been able to find comfort in that splendour or whether hunger and fear had drained them of their capacity to inspire. Reaching the saddle of the mountain, Nikos unshouldered his pack and lyra.

'Just there is the entrance to the Gorge of Tripitis. We will spend the night on the mountain before going down the canyon tomorrow.'

Stretching his back, the young Cretan stared around him. Above was the summit of Gigilos and to the north they could see right across the island to the coast. Beneath them the Libyan Sea reached out to the horizon, a tiny island way out to sea the only landfall between them and Africa.

'The little island is Gavdos,' Nikos told her pointing. 'It is about twenty-five miles away. It's the most southerly point in Europe and is part of Crete.'

'Do people live there?' asked Sarah.

'About fifty all year round, but in the summer months more people go out to work in tourism. A few thousand visitors who want to get away from it all visit in the high season. I have never been, but my grandfather lived there for a time.'

161

'Your grandfather, what did he do there?' Sarah could see Nikos hesitate.

'Is he still alive?'

'Yes, my *pappous* is alive but very old now. He lives and works in a village outside of Chania.' Despite himself Nikos found it difficult not to open up to Sarah.

'He still works?' Sarah tried to calculate out how old Nikos' granddad might be.

'He will never stop until they put him in a casket.' Nikos laughed.

'What does he do?'

He had come so far, there could be no harm in answering Sarah's questions and it felt good to Nikos to talk about his *pappous*.

'He is a musician and luthier, he makes lyras, like mine.' A reluctant Nikos answered. This was getting more personal and to close to the mess of his family life that he had wanted to keep to himself. He saw Sarah was digesting the remarkable coincidence that both their grandfathers were musicians.

'So playing lyra runs in the family, that's where you get your talent. Is he your dad's or your mum's parent?'

'He's my mother's father, my own father died when I was two. Granddad and my mother don't get on. They don't see each other or even speak on the phone. Would you like to climb to the summit?' Nikos changed the subject.

Sarah understood that Nikos had again slammed the door closed on the conversation, recognising how uncomfortable he felt giving so much of himself away.

'It looks steep?' Sarah gazed at the peak above and the rocky side of the mountain she would need to traverse to reach its summit.

'It looks worse than it is, and the view from the top is wonderful.'

Turning, he held out his hand for Sarah to follow.

There was no real path, just a way sporadically marked with red and yellow blobs of paint. But the ground was solid under-foot and after an hour of walking and scrambling on all fours they crested the summit. If the view from the saddle of the mountain had been beautiful, from here it was sublime. It was like standing on top of the world. Nikos pointed out the Samaria Gorge, and the city of Chania to the north glistening in the sun beside the Aegean Sea. To the south the higher peak of Mount Volakias rose above them, and the view out across the Libyan Sea to Gavdos Sarah thought was peerless.

Seeing the offshore island again, Sarah wondered if she should ask the question which had been playing on her mind.

'What did your granddad do on Gavdos?' Curiosity had got the better of her.

Nikos hesitated, then spoke. 'He was an exile.' The comment hung in the air like an eagle poised to swoop. 'Shall we go down, light a fire and make ourselves comfortable for the night?'

Loath to leave it there, Sarah was wise enough to be patient. She sensed Nikos had already given away more about himself than he intended, but bit by bit she might be able to discover why he would not teach her the lyra.

Nikos laid out some blankets in the shelter of an old sheep pen and set about gathering wood for a fire. While he searched down the mountain, Sarah sat gazing out on this mystical landscape and contemplated where this journey that had started in a cottage in England had brought her. In Nikos she felt she had found a man who she could love and who would love her, but there was something he was holding back. If she pressed him to reveal too much she was in danger of losing him but she could not have a relationship with a man who kept secrets.

As he descended to the tree line in search of wood, Nikos pondered the dilemma in which he found himself. Few people knew the family history that had brought him to where he was now in his life and the inner pain that caused him. It had felt good letting go that little bit with Sarah. What harm would it do to give more of himself? Perhaps it would help him feel better. It was not as though he would see her again after these few days were over.

Lighting the fire, Nikos took a foil package from his backpack, placing it on the warm embers to the side of the fire. '*Kleftico*, are you hungry?'

Sarah nodded.

'It usually takes hours to cook, but I prepared and baked it back at my uncle's house so it shouldn't take so long.' Nikos settled back on a blanket and, pulling a bottle of wine and two tumblers from his rucksack, he poured a glass for each of them.

As dusk fell the only light they could see was a sky of stars glinting. The *kleftico* was a dish of tender lamb slow-cooked in a sauce of olive oil, onion, garlic, tomatoes and lemon along with potatoes baked in the juices and dotted with goats' cheese. Sated with the food and relaxed by the wine, Sarah found the fortitude to probe further.

'Why was your granddad in exile?'

He had known the question would come at some stage. In that moment Nikos took the decision and began to tell his grandfather's story.'

'He was arrested by soldiers of the military dictatorship after the coup of 1967.'

Sarah's mouth dropped in amazement at what Nikos was telling her.

'Somehow he managed to escape the clutches of the Junta, he had been an andarte during the Second World War and knew the mountains like the back of his hand. But hiding out on Crete was dangerous. Supporters of the regime were always likely to give away his whereabouts. Making his way to Paleochora, he found a fisherman willing to take him to Gavdos. He hid out there until news reached him that the colonels had been toppled in 1974. That's about it really.'

'What had he done that the regime wanted to put him in prison?' Sarah was keen to learn more.

'Playing songs. He was arrested for playing songs of the Resistance.'

'They imprisoned people for making music?' Sarah looked incredulous.

'That is all. I know it is hard to believe. It was illegal to play music the junta felt was unsympathetic to their regime. When he escaped to Gavdos they took everything. They closed down his business and sold the property in Chania. My grandmother and mother were left with nothing. My grandmother died of a heart attack whilst her husband was still in exile. Mother was left to fend for herself. She was a teenager when my *pappous* went into hiding and a young woman by the time he returned.'

'He was a Resistance fighter during the war?' Sarah interrupted.

'All I know is what my mother has told me and she doesn't know much. Granddad never talks about it. The Nazis murdered his parents in a reprisal raid on his village. Their death and the civil war that followed the German withdrawal from the island both left their scars. I think he tries his best to forget those times.'

As Nikos reached out to move his lyra closer, Sarah was torn. She wanted to hear more about his grandfather but also longed to hear Nikos play again. If she pushed him further maybe he would shut down.

In the dark of the mountains, Nikos' playing took on a new dimension. It was as if it claimed the stars, the mountains and the far off sea as its own and embraced all the hardships and pain suffered by the remarkable people of this endlessly intriguing island.

'Now you,' Nikos handed the instrument to Sarah who longed to play but felt hesitant performing in front of her accomplished companion.

'You say your grandfather made this.' She turned the lyra through her hands. The body was of a lighter colour than her instrument and the fingerboard was inlaid with what looked to be shells. Unlike hers, the bird carved on the body appeared to be a dove rather than an eagle.

'He made it with me. He not only taught me how to play but he wanted me to become a master craftsman like him. He would like me to take over the business when he dies. Until a couple of years ago I would often work with him, but now that is impossible. I do not have the time as I need to work in my mother's taverna.'

Nikos nodded encouragement to Sarah in an attempt to move away from a subject he found uncomfortable. 'Play.'

As she drew the bow across the strings, Sarah sensed a freedom in her playing she had not experienced before. The joy at the beginnings of love and the pain of what Nikos was keeping from her all came out in the music. As they took it in turns to play, she began to understand what Yannis had meant about the lyra being the spirit of Crete. Sitting on that mountainside beneath the star-studded sky it felt as though they were the only two people on earth. That night they made love under the stars warmed by the closeness of their bodies and the dying embers of the fire.

The sharp edge of a chilly dawn roused Sarah. Nikos was already up, rekindling the fire to boil water for coffee. He was keen to make an early start on their descent of the gorge. Sarah felt she would like this time alone with Nikos to last forever. Who knew what the future might bring when they got off the mountain?

Squeezing through the narrowest of gaps in the rocks, the couple entered the head of the Gorge of Tripitis. Nikos warned that inexperienced walkers sometimes got wedged between the sides and some had even died after becoming trapped. The young Cretan was sure-footed but Sarah had to keep her wits about her as they scrambled down the steep incline into the heart of the gorge.

At first the couple descended in contented solitude but as their thoughts encroached on the silence, both began to feel uneasy. Where would their relationship stand when they got to Paleochora? Sarah felt her insecurities rising. She had already given enough of herself that she was terrified of getting hurt. Nikos was also in turmoil: he had fallen harder than he thought for the young Englishwoman. Perhaps if he told her the truth about how his life was, he could let her down gently.

Sarah was first to break the silence. She could not go on without finding out why Nikos was so reluctant to talk about himself.

'Do you enjoy working in the taverna?'

'It is difficult, I have no choice. My mother runs it but she is not so young and I have to work so she can pay the rent. I am trying to build the business as we have not had it long, but it is difficult in the recession, the government are always asking for more tax, they take all we have. It should have been so different.'

'What do you mean?' Sarah sensed she was getting to the heart of the story.

'My mother was an English teacher; she knows nothing about running a business.'

Nikos held out a hand to help Sarah over a boulder blocking their path.

'Her pension has been slashed by the government because of the financial crisis. She hasn't enough to live on. She is a widow and if I don't work she will lose the taverna and will starve. She does not talk to my grandfather, so I am the only person she has in the world who she can rely on.'

Sarah stopped for a moment.

'Do you still see your grandfather?'

'Only in secret. She blames him for her situation. They had a strained enough relationship before the crash but since her financial problems they have become estranged. I partly blame myself for that.'

Sarah could see Nikos was struggling. She motioned for him to sit next to her on a rock. 'Why's that?' she coaxed gently.

'They both see a different future for me. Until the financial meltdown mother could afford to indulge me working with my grandfather and playing lyra for a living. She hated anything to do with music as she blamed it for the family losing everything as well as the death of her mother when my *pappous* was in exile.

'She is an intelligent woman but cannot see that I can support us making lyras and teaching and playing music. She associates all that with the old ways that have got the country in such a state, and why my grandfather was exiled and the family lost everything. Even if I had the time she wouldn't let me pursue that course. She is so determined to put blame on my granddad that she is blind to reason.

'She has it in her head that tourism is the only way forward but she has no experience of ordering produce, cooking or any of the things the taverna entails. With me working all hours we just about keep our heads above water but she is getting too old to work like that and I grow more and more resentful of the situation as time goes on.'

Speaking about his problems to Sarah had not helped ease the hopelessness he felt. Even the sight of a pair of kri-kri grazing in a glade between the pine trees could not lift their spirits and Sarah regretted pushing Nikos to talk.

'I'm sorry, I shouldn't have asked,' Sarah took Nikos' hand. 'It's not your fault,' he replied, 'and I am ruining our day.' As he looked down, Sarah took his head in her hands and kissed him. In that moment they both sensed there could be a future for them. Stopping for a drink and a snack Nikos took out the lyra and played, the music embracing the melancholy of their mood and soothing the spirit.

'You must never stop playing,' whispered Sarah.

As they continued through the canyon Nikos pointed out the numerous caves chiselled out of the limestone. It was in one of these that Sarah's grandfather would have hidden before heading for the beach to make his rendezvous with the boat that was to take him off the island.

Emotionally drained and physically exhausted, as the sun reached its zenith the couple found their way to the mouth of the gorge. The pebble beach was strewn with huge boulders as if thrown there in a game of five-stones played by the gods. Barely a ripple troubled the surface as they stripped off and dived into the water. Floating in the Libyan Sea, Sarah pondered how this benign spot must have felt to her grandfather in danger, awaiting rescue in the dark?

She had now tracked the course taken by John during the war, but felt the lyra was still leading her towards another phase of her life. She knew her future with Nikos was filled with confusion but she would follow the course of this adventure to its conclusion, wherever it might take her.

The dive boat grew larger as it sped towards them and the couple rushed to dress and await their liberation from the beach. As they waded out to the inflatable, Lefteris helped them aboard and Georgos handed them each a bottle of beer from the cold box. Reversing off the shore, the rib was soon skimming the surface of the water in the direction of Paleochora. Georgos at the helm pointed out the long beach of the isolated village of Sougia as they sped past.

A shout from the bow got Sarah's attention and following Lefteris pointed finger she caught sight of a dolphin breaking the surface. It was joined by eight or nine others as the pod played in the bow wave before diving one last time and disappearing for good.

Nikos' uncle owned a taverna and pension by the beach on the west side of town. Sarah was made welcome and shown to a room with a balcony looking out on the Libyan Sea. As the sun set they sat at a table weighed down with *mezzes*. Lefteris and Georgos enjoined Nikos to play and soon the trio was performing an informal concert. As they played, customers got up to dance and waiters moved tables aside to create a dancefloor.

When Nikos held out the lyra to Sarah, to the amazement of the dancers, she did not hesitate to take over the playing. Traffic stopped as the dancers formed a line that spilled out onto the road and drivers wound down their windows to shout encouragement. Watching her play, Nikos was sure of one thing at last, he could not let this woman escape his life. If he was to find happiness he would have to follow his own path and see where it would take him.

It was the early hours by the time Nikos and Sarah found themselves alone at the table. It was agreed that the next morning she would return by ferry to Agia Roumeli and then on to Chora Sfakion to pick up her luggage before taking the return journey to

Paleochora the following day. Although unsure what the future held, they were now both certain that it should be together.

After an all too short night with Sarah in his arms, Nikos was reluctant to watch his girlfriend sail away from Paleochora quay. They both knew that the sooner she departed the sooner she would return and they could be together. Although Nikos had taken the plunge with this unspoken commitment, the problem of his own future remained unresolved. He badly needed the two days they would be apart to consider how to confront his mother. He knew it would not be easy but if he was going to hold on to the girl he had fallen for it was something he had to meet head on.

For Sarah the next two days could not pass quickly enough. The most beautiful of spring days showed off the coastal landscape to perfection. As she took the two ferry journeys back to Chora Sfakion she was too happy at the prospect of what her relationship with Nikos held to fully appreciate the wonders of nature that surrounded her. The following day, loaded with her luggage, her mood had not changed. She could not remember being this happy since before the death of her granddad. The skipper of *Neptune* greeted her as she boarded his boat for the trip to Agia Roumeli, where she would await the connecting ferry to take her back to Paleochora.

As the boat approached the quay at Agia Roumeli, groups of walkers wanting to experience the Samaria Gorge without walking the whole length from the top eagerly awaited to disembark. Sarah thought back to when she had arrived at this same spot just four days before and how much her life had changed since then. She let the enthusiastic trekkers push past before stepping off the boat to find a taverna with a view of the quay where she could sit and await the ferry which would take her back to Nikos in Paleochora.

After the walkers dispersed, the village returned to a state of blissful tranquillity. Sarah gazed out to sea, sipping at an iced coffee whilst searching the horizon. She closed her eyes as the sun warmed her face and said a silent thank you to her granddad who had guided her throughout life and in the end had left her the lyra that had led her to Crete and the man she was in love with.

Her lyra, violin and holdall safely at her feet, Sarah watched as the vessel *Samaria I* moored and disgorged it passengers. She had time to kill before the ferry departed in the late afternoon but she was content to read, maybe later she would swim. The flurry of activity on the quay over as passengers were dispatched, those going about their day-to-day business being absorbed into the village streets, Sarah returned her attention to her book. She did not notice the woman approach until she spoke.

'You are the Englishwoman my brother-in-law told me about who plays lyra,' she said, looking down at her instrument cases it was more of a statement than a question.

Sarah smiled as she looked up from her book, but the woman dressed in black widow's weeds did not return the friendly look. Staring into the eyes of this formidable small woman, everything about her filled Sarah with disquiet.

'You should get back on the next boat to Chora Sfakion. My son has already left Paleochora and will not return anytime soon. He has gone back to Kalyves where he belongs, to see his fiancée.'

The words hit Sarah like a gunshot. Nikos' mother showed no emotion as she delivered the news that threw Sarah's life into turmoil. The hint of a smile lifted the corner of the woman's mouth as she turned and walked away. Meanwhile a tear traced its course down Sarah's cheek. She found it impossible to stem the flood as she gave in to her grief. The bright future, which only moments before had seemed to hold so much for her, had been ripped away, replaced by a fog of confusion and hurt.

Exhausted and aching with crying, the sun dried the last of her tears as *Neptune* drew away from the quay heading east, back to Chora Sfakion. What she would do now she hadn't a clue. She reached for her mobile and sent the text to Nikos. 'It's over. I never want to see you again.'

Chapter 10

THAT DAY WHEN Vassilis led John towards his rendezvous on the beach, a German patrol was spotted heading up Gigilos and a group of Resistance fighters had been hastily dispatched to stalk them and ensure that the Englishman reached his target safely. The Germans had a head start, but the andarte knew the mountains.

In agony with his shattered leg, Vassilis could see the rest of the German squad spreading out to draw his fire. He knew he could only keep them at bay for a short time. Firing again, he tried to buy his friend more time to escape. *Eleftheria y thanatos*, he would try to live up to those departing words left by his English comrade. He took another slug of raki from his flask to dull the pain and took aim.

He saw the German soldier fall back, swung his rifle round and aimed at another who had broken cover. The shot missed but sent its target scuttling behind a rock. He tried to count the number of enemy coming for him. It didn't matter, he told himself, on the ledge he was a sitting duck. Another shot hit the rock behind his head and instinct told him to lie down. Every move he took was agony but, crying out in pain, he dragged his leg round and flopped to the ground. From the prone position, he took aim and fired at the lead German but his head felt dizzy and he could not see if it had made its mark. A salvo of fire rang out and everything went black.

'Don't talk. We'll get you out of here.'

The pain was excruciating. Vassilis reached for his flask of raki. It was empty.

'We poured it on your injured leg,' said the voice.

Glancing down, the wounded Cretan could see his leg strapped to a makeshift splint and a tourniquet tied around his thigh.

'Here, I have some,' he heard another voice, and a flask was put to his lips. The fiery liquid burned his parched throat before it worked its magic and he fell unconscious.

The andarte had caught their prey just as the first shots were fired at Vassilis and John. Taking the Germans by surprise they had been easy targets for the Cretans to pick off.

It was fortunate for Vassilis that he knew little about the tortuous three-day journey back through Tripitis Gorge, down the slopes of Mount Gigilos to the Omalos Plateau and the relative safety of Samaria Gorge. It took all of the four andarte who had saved his life to carry the stretcher they had fashioned out of wood from the trees and the clothes from their backs.

Still it was touch and go whether Vassilis would make it. For three days more he tossed and turned in his bed, drifting in and out of consciousness. It was a full week after his ordeal on the ledge outside the cave before he learned of his miraculous escape from death.

In the coming days, Vassilis grew stronger. Under the ministrations of the local doctor his leg slowly mended. It was a year before he was fully mobile and a further six months before his leg was strong enough to carry him any distance. During that time the Germans became more desperate and ruthless in their reprisals against the Cretans whose spirit they had failed to break. The British were dropping weapons to arm the andarte and Special Forces were landed on the island and working alongside the Resistance to cause maximum disruption to the occupying regime.

Angry at the refusal of the proud Cretan people to kowtow to Nazi jurisdiction, the Germans slaughtered innocent civilians in their thousands. The murder of his parents, executed alongside the others in his village in a reprisal raid by the Nazis, had a profound effect on the young Cretan. The litany of death that continued as Greeks turned on each other in the Civil War that followed further took its toll. More than fifty thousand people lost their lives across the whole of Greece in that conflict.

When Vassilis returned to his village, he sought to draw a veil over his past. Although seen as a war hero, he chose to forget his act of bravery and found solace in his music and crafting the lyras he so loved. When playing, his mind would escape to the mountains, valleys and beaches of the land of his birth and in chiselling, planing and sanding the wood to craft an instrument, he could create a lasting legacy.

Through the years of neglecting his art, Vassilis' skills had not diminished. If anything, he nurtured the instruments he made more and his playing became imbued with the richness of his tragic past. Performers would come from across the island and sometimes elsewhere in Greece to commission lyras from him. Instead of an eagle, the luthier now lovingly sculpted a dove of peace on the back of every instrument he made.

Nikos stared at the screen of his mobile phone in disbelief. It was only a matter of hours before they were due to meet up again and Sara had ditched him. He tried to call her but the number was blocked. How could he have misjudged how she felt about him so badly? Rumours travelled fast on Crete, was it possible she had heard something about one of his many past relationships from someone in Chora Sfakion? But they were just dalliances, while in Sarah he truly believed he had found love. He had already steeled himself to tell his mother he wanted to be with Sarah and to teach, play and make lyras. If they worked hard, he felt sure they could make enough money to support her and themselves.

One thing was certain, now that he had found Sarah he would not let her go without a fight. He must at least find her so he could understand why she had put an end to their relationship. There were no more ferries out of Paleochora that day: if she was in Agia Roumeli he could only get there by descending Samaria Gorge but it shut at dusk. It was more likely that she was in Chora Sfakion if she had not packed her bags and fled elsewhere. If he could borrow a car from Lefteris or Georgos he could take the long drive all the way across the island to Chania then back around the other side of the Lefka Ori to Chora Sfakion. When he phoned, Lefteris was out on the boat.

'You can take the van, the keys are under the stone by the door to our container at the harbour, but if you can wait until tomorrow we could take you by boat,' offered Lefteris.

Nikos was convinced time was of the essence, 'I think I'll take the van if that's OK? Thanks.'

Nikos did the best he could to coax the reluctant vehicle, rickety and heavy with diving tanks and other paraphernalia, around the hairpin bends, going as fast as he dared on the mountain roads which criss-crossed the island. What if she had already left?

Sarah sat at one of the tables on the waterfront. The owner of the taverna was surprised to see her back but only too pleased for her to rebook the room. She had ordered rabbit stifado but even the aroma of the deep red wine sauce flavoured with garlic, cinnamon and tomatoes could not tempt her jaded appetite. The glass of wine she toyed with had lost its appeal. Knowing she had to work out what to do next, she couldn't steady her thoughts enough to make any plans. First Gareth and now Nikos, what was wrong with her choices in men? With her ex-fiancé, after he had cheated on her Sarah felt she had a lucky escape. With Nikos she felt distraught. She had been sure that he was the love of her life, and the betrayal made her fall to earth much harder.

The taverna owner could see Sarah was upset. He was fond of the Englishwoman. Unsure if he should impose on her grief, sympathy and intrigue overcame his reluctance enough for him to intervene.

'Did I see you had a lyra with you in your luggage?'

Sarah looked up from pushing food around her plate and nodded.

'And you play?'

'I am learning slowly,' replied Sarah modestly, not sure whether she wanted conversation.

'Then you must play now, it will help take the pain away. I'll go and get some raki for us to share and you can play for me. You'll see, it will make you feel better, trust me.'

While he went to get the drinks Sarah returned to her room for the lyra. Back at the table she ran the bow through the block of rosin before tentatively drawing it across the strings. In an instant her thoughts cleared as her absorption in the music transformed her distress to melancholy.

'I thought you said you were learning slowly.' Her new friend sat down, placing the raki and glasses between them.

Sarah smiled; he had been right. The lyra had a healing effect on her soul and as she played all her sadness flowed out in the music.

Nikos prayed he was not too late as he slung the van into a parking space on the roundabout near the memorial. How would he find Sarah? That is, if she was still here. He had no idea where she was staying.

Stepping from the van, his ears were immediately attuned to a sound with which he was familiar. Softly floating in time to the Libyan Sea caressing the beach, he followed the melody as if it were leading him from the labyrinth.

When he saw Sarah sitting at the table playing he had never been more certain of anything in his life. For a moment, he watched and listened as the woman he loved played. Whatever had come between them, somehow he must unravel this mess and make her stay.

Afraid to break the spell, in the shadows of a nearby taverna he stood unnoticed as the music went round and round in his head, rising and falling softly then louder, etching indelible patterns on his mind until reaching a crescendo. Sarah lifted the bow from the strings.

'Bravo,' the man sitting opposite shouted and began to clap.

'Bravo,' Nikos stepped out of the shadow and joined the lonely applause.

Sarah felt the trace of a smile reach her eyes before the anger she felt at her betrayal hardened her features.

'What are you doing here?'

'I came to ask you to marry me.'

'Won't your fiancée have something to say about that?'

'What are you talking about?' Nikos faltered as he recognised the hand of his mother in his lover's sudden disappearance.

'I promise there is no-one else. Who told you that?'

The taverna owner stood, signalled for Nikos to sit and disappeared inside his restaurant. Nikos' eyes enquired whether he should take the chair. Sarah nodded, before telling how his mother had intercepted her at Agia Roumeli and warned her that he was engaged and she should leave.

'Mother must have heard about us from my uncle, her brother-in-law, they speak on the phone every day. She wants me to marry a girl I went to school with whose parents own a hotel next to her taverna. It will never happen. We are good friends but that is all. She has a boyfriend who she loves and anyway I am not attracted to her. My mother has got it in her head that we will marry, that the hotel will then come into our family and she will have no more money worries and I will give up on my ambition to work with my grandfather. Please Sarah, trust what I am telling you is true.'

The emotional turmoil of the day had left Sarah speechless. Whether her tears were of relief or anger, she did not know. In her heart she believed Nikos, but his earlier evasiveness and the interference of his mother in their relationship had scared her and made her wary. Her silence and tears filled Nikos with fear that he was losing her, especially when she brushed off the arm he reached around her.

'That is the last time she will interfere in my life. I have to go.' Nikos turned and left. Before Sarah could see through the fog of her tears and confusion, he had gone. Should she go after him? Was she letting this man slip through her fingers – why was she sitting rooted to the chair?

'May I?' Without waiting for a response, the owner of the taverna took the chair vacated by Nikos placing another *carafaki* of raki on the table in front of them.

'What time does the first bus to Chania leave in the morning?' Sarah asked wiping her eyes on her sleeve.

'You are not leaving? You are upset. You belong here on Crete. You forget so soon, I have listened to you play. Go to Loutro for a few days; take your lyra.' The taverna owner pulled a handful of napkins from the holder on the table and offered them to Sarah.

It was dark as Nikos jammed the van into gear and retraced his route back towards Chania. If his previous journey had been fuelled by fear that the woman he loved would have left, this one was driven by anger. How could his mother have interfered in his life in such a way? He was no longer prepared to let her dictate his future and he was determined to tell her that, whatever the consequences.

As he came to a halt outside the taverna in Kalyves, the dim lights were still on but there were no customers. Nikos could make out the dark shadow of his mother still sitting in the back of the restaurant. Striding through the tables and chairs on the terrace he was determined to get his words out first.

'What do you mean interfering in my life like that!' shouted Nikos.

'What do you mean?' Nikos did not buy his mother's incredulity.

'You know all too well what I am talking about. How dare you tell the woman I love that I am engaged to another woman.'

'The woman you love. A foreigner, and a musician as well. Don't you love me? It was for your own good, it would only end in our ruin. Isn't your grandfather a good enough example of where this obsession with music leads.' His mother's rant continued. 'I gave up everything for you, and this is all the thanks I get. Running off with a foreigner, thinking nothing of what will become of me. Well I won't let her steal you! I saw her face when I told her you were engaged, she'll be long gone by now.'

'No mother, she is not long gone. I have found her. By doing this you have ruined our family. We could have worked things out if you hadn't interfered. But you cannot help yourself. I will not let you ruin my life anymore.' Turning, Nikos made his way back to the car. 'Goodbye mother. You'll have to sort things out for yourself now.'

Lying in bed, Sarah was restless, her mind churning. She tried to piece together what had brought her here. Was it to help heal the heartbreak of her grandfathers' death; to recover from the breakup of a relationship she now realised she was lucky to have escaped? What was there for her back in England now? The one thing that remained constant was the lyra left to her by her granddad. He had never let her down and she loved playing the magical instrument. Maybe the taverna owner was right: take some time, go to Loutro, perhaps play some music and see where life would take her. 'Go on and conquer the world' – her granddad's words again strengthened her resolve.

A flying fish leaped clear of the water, a cat rolled over to warm its other side on the coach roof of the *Neptune* as its wake ploughed a furrow across a field of cobalt blue. Whether it was fatigue or the boundless beauty of the landscape as the ferry sailed westwards Sarah did not know, but her anxiety had given way to contentment. Somehow she managed to anchor her thoughts in the present and let the healing powers of the sun and sea work their miracles.

It seemed more than a week since she had set foot in the secluded village, as she returned to the same pension. Hardly having eaten the night before, she was hungry and went back to the familiar taverna by the beach, and ordered breakfast. Gazing towards the mountains to the east of the village Sarah's eyes were drawn towards a track traversing the cliffs.

'*Glyca Nera*. Sweetwater Bay. The track leads there,' said the waiter, answering Sarah's unasked question. 'It's a bit of a walk, but the beach is beautiful.'

The thought of a walk appealed to Sarah. It would be a chance to be alone with her thoughts. She returned to her room and changed into walking boots, applied sun cream and put her swimming gear and a couple of bottles of water in her pack.

Leaving the village she set off uphill along the path she had seen from the taverna.

The trek along the cliffside was arduous but the views were extraordinary. She passed the gleaming white chapel she had spotted from *Neptune* the week before, and marvelled at how the materials to build it had been brought up the mountainside. She fondly remembered how Nikos had told her that the higher and more difficult these churches were to build, the more the rich patrons who paid for them believed their sins would be absolved as the chapels were closer to heaven.

The sun got hotter as she walked and Sarah dropped her pace. Stopping to quench her thirst, she looked back and forward along the path. As far as she could see, she was alone on the mountainside. The aroma of wild sage brought back memories of her trek up the Samaria Gorge with Nikos just a week before.

The descent to the isolated pebble shore was welcome. The taverna built out over the sea with a jetty where water taxis could moor was still boarded up. A line of stunted trees grew out of the beach that lay beneath the White Mountains precariously poised above. Sarah looked around. She was alone on the beach. Changing into her swimming costume she waded out into the gin clear bay. Diving in to the freezing water took her breath away and she could feel beneath her feet the strange sensation of cold water bubbling up through the seabed. Refreshed, she lay on the beach to dry in the sun.

The walk back to Loutro had worked up an appetite, and she headed straight to the taverna. Sarah was grateful to the waiter for warning her off ordering too many dishes from his menu. Looking out to sea in the warmth of the afternoon sun, Sarah could feel Loutro working its magic. A ferry carrying exhausted trekkers from the Samaria Gorge briefly docked but no passengers disembarked. On the horizon a speedboat bounced across the water as the sun dropped lower in the sky in the direction of Agia Roumeli.

Still exhausted from not sleeping the night before, Nikos welcomed the cool spray from the bow wave. Whatever the outcome, the events of the last twenty-four hours would change his life forever. His mother had been shocked at his anger and resolve but had refused to back down and apologise for her interference.

When he walked away, he felt sorry for her, now estranged not only from her father but from her only son. Driving back across the island to Paleochora his resentment had diminished as the miles between them increased but he had never been more certain of anything. He wanted to spend the rest of his life with Sarah and if his relationship with his mother had to suffer, then so be it.

He had one errand to run before meeting with Lefteris and Georgos at their berth in the harbour. True to their word, the two friends were waiting in the dive boat. Georgos opened the throttle as the vessel left behind the harbour mouth and turned the wheel to an easterly heading.

If Nikos had been a bundle of nerves before they moored up at Chora Sfakion, discovering that Sarah had left for Loutro increased the apprehension he felt to fever pitch. The longer before he saw her, the more he played out every scenario in his mind and by the time they sped past the island protecting the mouth of the small bay he could hardly speak.

When the boat moored up on the other side of the quay, Sarah watched as only one of the three-man crew hauled themselves onto the dockside. While two men busied themselves tying ropes, the third made his way towards the tavernas that lined the beach where Sarah was sitting. His stance looked stooped and his steps unsure but as he got closer he was unmistakable. As she recognised the figure of Nikos walking towards her, he in turn saw Sarah sitting in the same place that he had set eyes on her little more than a week before. If Sarah mouthed a greeting he heard nothing, so concentrated was he on getting his words out. Encouraged by the slight upturn of her mouth, he reached in his pocket.

'Marry me.' The words escaped not as a question or command but more of a plea from this strong man who had led her through the mountains. Struggling he opened the small box he was holding.

Sarah would never remember which came first, her tears or the answer 'yes' she had managed to gasp. Holding out her hand to

191

Nikos, she was sure she had just made the most important decision of her life. As they wrapped their arms around each other neither noticed Lefteris, Georgos or the waiter break into applause. By the time they let each other go, a bottle of champagne had found its way to the table. The cork popped and toasts were made to the couple's future.

As more drinks were brought, Nikos quietly related the story of his confrontation with his mother. He was sure that his grandfather would welcome him back to his workshop and that he could now pursue his dream. If there was anything impinging on the elation Sarah now felt, she put it to the back of her mind, nothing was going to spoil this night, she raised her glass. 'To granddad and the lost lyra.'

Chapter 11

SARAH TRIED NOT to be disappointed that Liz was unable to come to the wedding. As she had no family, and because Nikos and his mother were estranged, there was little to delay the ceremony once the required bureaucracy had been dealt with. Unlike most Cretan weddings, theirs was to be a modest affair, celebrated as soon as arrangements could be made with a priest. Sarah phoned Liz to invite her but at such short notice she was unable to get away from work, being due to present a new range of dishes to her bosses, but she promised to go to the cottage, find Sarah's birth certificate and forward it to Crete. Liz was happy that Sarah had at last found happiness and sad that she could not be there for her. Sarah phoned Douglas to let him know her news, and the elderly man was delighted but, as she had suspected, would be unable to make the journey.

It was decided the wedding would take place in the village of Nikos' *pappous'* in the foothills of the White Mountains to the south of Chania. As Nikos had hoped, his grandfather had welcomed him back into his business with open arms. He was proud of his grandson's talent, both as a luthier and a musician. His prayers were answered and his legacy would continue. Whoever this young English girl was, he was happy Nikos had found her. Why did his own daughter hate so much the music that he loved? It hurt him to think how far apart they had grown but now he could at least find solace in his grandson's future. Shortly after hearing news of his engagement, Nikos was surprised when his grandfather announced he was going to Athens on business, but had assured him he would be back for the wedding day. The owner of the taverna had been only too pleased to host the wedding celebrations and the local priest said he would be honoured to perform the ceremony. Speaking little Greek, Sarah had been more than happy when her fiancé had suggested he handle all the arrangements for their big day.

As the wedding drew closer, Sarah became aware of something dulling the edge of her happiness. She knew the sacrifice Nikos had made to be with her. Although his future now held so much of what he had longed for, she understood more than most the pain of living without a parent in her life. In his anger, Nikos believed his mother was hard and uncaring. Despite the appearances Sarah had got from their one and only encounter, she believed his mother had acted through fear. She was afraid she would lose her son to the music which had taken her father from her; she was afraid that she would lose her son to a foreign woman she did not know; and she was afraid that she would lose her livelihood and home.

Whilst Nikos was absorbed in making preparations, Sarah realised that when life settled down into its day-to-day routine, it would not be so easy for him to wipe his mother from his memory. If there was anything she could do to make them reconcile, she was determined to try.

From Chania, Sarah caught a bus to Souda Bay, out past the Allied War Cemetery she had visited the day she first arrived in the west of the island. Freighters lay at anchor in the lagoon, and an incoming ferry from Athens crossed course with a warship heading seawards. Inland, holiday villas dotted the hills and along the roadside tavernas, bars, studios and souvenir shops were opening and already providing for the early season holiday trade. This was Kalyves. If the development along the main road through the resort was unremarkable, the small square with a church through which Sarah cut down to the seafront was delightful.

The beach reached in both directions, stretching out to a small harbour at its eastern end. The seafront tavernas and cafes were doing a sluggish trade but it was not difficult for Sarah to find Nikos' mother's business. It was empty, the tables unlaid and no menu at the entrance. To all intents and purposes it looked shut. Most people would have passed by, not noticing the woman sitting alone at a table at the back of the terrace.

When they had met in Agia Roumeli, Nikos' mother had appeared formidable despite her small stature. The woman Sarah now found was diminished by despair. Frail and unkempt, she did not rise from her seat as Sarah approached. The young Englishwoman could see the mother of the man she loved was broken.

She did not even resist when Sarah bent down and put her arms around her, but the damp seeping through Sarah's dress as she held her betrayed the welling up of the woman's emotions. Embarrassed by her tears, Nikos' mother released herself from Sarah's hug and dabbed at her face with a handkerchief.

'Can I get you a drink, a coffee or raki perhaps?' whispered the woman.

'That would be lovely, you sit there, let me get it. What would you like?' offered Sarah.

'*Nero, parakalo*. Water, please.'

196

Sarah disappeared inside to the bar and when she returned, Nikos' mother had calmed down.

'I'm Sarah.'

Hesitantly, the woman offered up her name also. 'Eleni.'

If she was going to build any bridges, Sarah knew she would have to lead the conversation with this embarrassed, scared and broken woman. Sarah talked of life back in England, the loss of her parents and how much her grandparents had meant to her. She told how her grandfather had fought in Crete and escaped from the island and how his life had been changed by the loss of his arm. Gradually Eleni warmed to the woman his son had chosen to marry. She knew she had treated her badly, but the guilt she felt made it difficult for her to get close to this girl who was showing her nothing but kindness.

As Sarah talked, she gently prompted Eleni to respond with her own story. Bit by bit, Nikos' mother opened up telling her about how she had lost her father to exile; the death of her husband and mother; how the crisis had stripped her of the security she had worked so hard to achieve. It had all poured out.

Sarah tried to reassure Eleni that her son loved her and that when they married they would be more than able to provide for her. The wedding could be a new start for all of them. As a family they could have a bright future together. Whatever had been said between Nikos and Eleni, she must come to the wedding.

Mention of the wedding struck fear into Eleni. Although she found it comforting to talk to Sarah, her altercation with her son and feud with her father were more deeply rooted. The prospect of seeing them both filled her with an anxiety she could not see a way to overcome. Sarah saw the fear in Eleni's eyes and did not push it further. As Sarah rose to leave, she noticed a hint of regret on the face of her future mother-in-law. She felt she had begun to build some bridges, but that it would take time to heal the hurt that ran so deep.

The days before the wedding were filled with little but excitement. The bride-to-be had bought a dress from a shop in Chania. With no family or friends, many of the traditional Cretan pre-wedding traditions did not apply. Nikos had agreed with his grandfather that after they were married the couple would stay in his house. In the meantime, Sarah had rented a room in the village and spent those glorious last days before the ceremony walking in the surrounding hills or meandering the ancient streets around the Venetian harbour in nearby Chania.

Sarah rose early. The wedding was not until late afternoon but in the restlessness of the night she felt the tug of loneliness rousing her to face the morning. There was no doubt she was happy, but wished she had someone to share her big day. She looked at her belongings, a holdall, a violin and the lyra. It was too early to get into her bridal gown, and she dared not leave the room as the

198

village was tiny and it would be bad luck if Nikos were to see her. She tried to read, to play her lyra but could not settle. The fridge in the room was well-stocked with food but she could not eat, the hours were dragging and by ten o'clock she felt that time must have stood still altogether.

A knock shook her from her languor. Opening the door, she saw the owner of the apartment who smiled a greeting.

'How is the bride this morning? I have a visitor for you.'

As Liz stepped forward, Sarah fell into her friend's arms. 'I thought you couldn't come?' Half laughing and half crying with joy, she held tight to her oldest friend in the world.

'I couldn't, but I have and I've brought you this. Shall I open it?' Liz handed over the bottle she had been trying not to drop under the weight of her friend's embrace.

'I think that would be a great idea,' said Sarah, letting go of Liz and leading her into the room.

'I thought about it, and I couldn't miss my best friend's wedding. I didn't like my work that much so it was a good excuse to leave.'

'You resigned!'

'I told them to stuff their job. I wanted to come back to Crete anyway.'

The time now raced past as Sarah recounted her time on the island. So engrossed were the friends in conversation that when Liz pointed out the time to Sarah she had to rush to get into her dress and do her hair and makeup. Only minutes before her groom and his best man and followers were due to arrive to escort her to the church did Sarah declare herself ready. A tearful Liz gave her a hug as the knock came on the door.

Nikos was resplendent in traditional Cretan costume, his trousers tucked in long, shining boots and an open waistcoat over a white shirt and cummerbund. He was flanked by his best man Lefteris – and Georgos. A group of Nikos' friends stood outside on the village lane, waiting to accompany the couple to the church.

'You look beautiful,' whispered a glowing Nikos to his bride to be. 'I have a surprise for you.'

As Nikos raised his arm in the air, the familiar figure of Yannis, her lyra teacher from London, stepped out from the group waiting in the cobbled street. His grin matched Sarah's as he approached and gave her a hug, before turning to Liz and kissing her on the lips. Sarah's raised brow was answered by Liz's beaming face.

'I'll tell you later,' Liz promised.

'I am here to lead the wedding party and it is traditional that we play music. It would be an honour if you would allow me to perform on your lyra. It has led you all the way here, it is only fitting that it guides you to the church.'

200

'It would be a privilege.' A smiling Sarah ducked back inside and emerged carrying her precious instrument.

The surprise of her two friends turning up on her wedding day could not have made Sarah happier. As the church bells pealed, she walked towards the small chapel to marry the man she was certain she loved more than anyone in the world. She looked across at her best friend, who proudly watched the young Cretan playing the lyra. Sarah was amazed at the number of villagers who left their homes to follow the procession. On the steps of the chapel, Nikos handed her a bouquet of anemones, delphiniums and apple blossom. The church was packed inside, while outside crowds of well-wishers in their Sunday best spilled onto the street, smoking, talking loudly with each other and shouting greetings to the couple. Taking a deep breath to steady her nerves, she stepped through the doorway.

The ceremony flashed past. The priest blessed the rings before two gold crowns redolent with orange blossom and linked by a ribbon were passed three times above the heads of the bride and groom. Led by Lefteris, the couple promenaded around the altar three times before the priest said prayers and they emerged once again into the sunlight. The bells rang out once more and gunshots were fired in the air. As the church disgorged its congregation, in a dark corner just one person remained.

Nikos and Sarah stood outside the taverna to welcome their guests. It appeared as though the whole village had turned out to greet them. Georgos held a plate on which envelopes containing money were placed as gifts for the newly-married couple who were wished *'Na zisete'* or 'long life' as the queue moved slowly inside.

An elderly man moved into the line beside Nikos. His eyes sparkled and beneath an impressive moustache his smile was kindly.

'This is my *pappous*,' Nikos introduced his grandfather with some pride. 'I'm so pleased you made it back from Athens in time.'

'I wouldn't have missed it for the world.' The man stepped forward and took Sarah's hand before kissing her on each cheek.

'I have heard a lot about you. It is my pleasure to meet you at last and to welcome you to the family.'

Immediately Sarah could see Nikos in his grandfather's eyes and knew that they would be friends.

Carafes of wine weighed on the tables and waiters were already bringing out salads and a wealth of *mezzes*. As Sarah and Nikos entered the room his grandfather took a stool at the centre of the musicians and picked up his lyra. The guitar of Lefteris and the laouto of Georgos were joined by a fiddle, a bouzouki, and bagpipes.

With the lyra in his hands the old man shed the years. As soon as he began to play the opening song, in the beautiful sound emanating from the instrument on his knee and the way he looked, Sarah could see and hear glimpses of the man she had married. Cheers rang out as he warmed to the music, the guests knowing they were in the presence of a maestro. Nikos had warned Sarah that according to tradition she would open the reception by dancing with him, then his best man before dancing with his family members. He eased his new bride through the simple steps of a dance before Lefteris left the stage to play his best man's role. Then Nikos' uncle stepped forward to represent her husband's family.

Even trying to concentrate on the unfamiliar steps of the dances, Sarah could tell she was listening to a true master play. Looking up, she saw both her husband and Yannis staring in awe as the old man turned his lyra into a living thing as if animated by the god of music. Sarah felt wrung out when the dances stopped and at the last draw of grandfather's bow the room fell silent.

As Nikos' uncle left the floor, the circle of guests parted and a woman stepped forward. Sarah moved to meet her mother-in-law and tears overtook them both as Eleni's smiling father struck up another tune.

'Thank you for coming. May I call you mother?' Sarah held Eleni close.

'I'm sorry, I'm so sorry.' Eleni was struggling to keep control. In the background Sarah saw Nikos wipe a tear from his eye and led her mother-in-law from the dance floor into the arms of her son.

As they sat to eat, a place for Eleni was laid next to Sarah. Nikos had never seen his mother warm to someone as much as she did to his new wife, and could not remember the last time he had seen her smile. When her father took a break from playing, his glow at seeing his daughter's happiness went a long way to healing the rift between them. As the evening went on it got harder to get Nikos' *pappous* back on stage as he began to form a new bond with his estranged child. With the wine flowing, Nikos even thought he heard his mother joke that now she was landed with a family of lyra players she would have to learn to live with it!

Nikos introduced Yannis to the dais to replace his granddad in the band before being called on stage himself to perform. When the old man returned to the stage, there wasn't a dry eye in the crowded taverna when he dedicated a song to his daughter Eleni.

'And now, I hear my new granddaughter is something of a maestro herself, let's see if we can encourage her to the stage.' As Nikos' grandfather stood to vacate his seat at the front of the platform, Sarah was struck with nerves.

'You go girl!' Liz reassured her friend, slurring ever so slightly.

As she looked around for her lyra, Yannis passed it across the table. Walking towards the rest of the band Sarah could feel the tension taking hold of her. Everything about her granddad's lyra had led to this moment. She felt his spirit with her as she sat surrounded by her fellow musicians.

She bowed the first note and cheers rang around the taverna. The band was following what she played but soon fell into the rhythm. Gaining in confidence, she felt the instrument give voice to her joyous mood. She remembered the melancholy of playing in Chora Sfakion and now the happiness she expressed infected the whole room. Looking round she could see her new husband beaming with pride, her best friend Liz gazing into the eyes of her boyfriend Yannis, the beatific smile of Eleni and the surprise registered on the face of the old maestro.

The bride's performance got the loudest cheer of the evening. Shouts for more rang in her ears. But she noticed Nikos' grandfather still had a strange look on his face as he made his way to the platform.

'Please Sarah, may I see your lyra?'

Handing the instrument to her new grandfather, she watched him turn it in his hands.

'I thought I recognised the sound. Where did you get this?'

'My granddad left it in his attic when he died. He must have brought it back from Crete where he fought in the war.'

A tear welled up in the old man's eye, 'And was your granddad called John?'

For the first time, Vassilis felt able to open up to his family about his experiences during the war. Somehow the return of the first lyra he had ever crafted now in the possession of the talented granddaughter of the friend to whom he had given it all those years ago, had unlocked something in the old man's heart. As the night went on he unburdened himself of the secrets he had kept for so long, telling Sarah, Nikos and Eleni the whole story of those dark times. He fondly remembered his friendship with the young English commando and how he had taught him to play the lyra. He recounted those days hiding out in the White Mountains. How he had led John down the Tripitis Gorge and given his precious lyra to his friend when he thought he would die holding the enemy at bay to enable his comrade's escape. He recounted how he miraculously cheated death and his long battle back to health.

Sarah in turn told Vassilis about her grandfather's past and the importance he held in her life. She recalled what she knew about his heroism and horrific injuries, how his dreams were shattered, and how he had encouraged her to be a musician. She explained to Vassilis how, following her granddad's death, she had found the lyra in the trunk in the loft and how it had led her to Crete and to Nikos, Eleni and Vassilis himself. Somehow, the lyra the andarte had given away to John in that ultimate act of generosity had united their two families.

When all three generations retired exhausted to their beds as the dawn began to break, it was hard for any one of them to imagine they had ever been happier.

Chapter 12

THE DISCOVERY AT the wedding that the lyra had been given to her grandfather by Vassilis had brought an end to Sarah's quest to find out her grandfather's history on Crete. The evening following the wedding day, beneath a pergola draped in vine, the whole family, as well as Liz and Yannis, had gathered for a celebratory meal. The garden attached to Vassilis' workshop was filled with pots bursting with orange, red and white geraniums and a purple bougainvillea climbed the wall behind a large wooden dovecote supported on a pole. As the old man turned a goat on a spit, Sarah was keen to hear all about her two friends' burgeoning relationship and learned how they had got together after meeting whilst planning Sarah's trip. Yannis had finished his studies in England

and after Liz had resigned, she had decided to join her boyfriend back home in Crete.

Nikos was full of plans for their future. Marketing Cretan dance nights to tavernas and hotels across the island, giving private lessons on the lyra and building a website to sell the instruments he and his granddad would hand craft in the workshop. Sarah intended to join him performing on the lyra and the violin and teaching both instruments and Yannis was also keen to join in with the venture. She would rent out the home her grandfather had left her in England to give them some income until they got established.

One person remained quiet. Eleni had been reassured by her son that between them they would look after her. Despite Nikos' reassurances, his mother was acutely aware how precarious the lives of musicians could be. Nothing had made her happier than the reconciliation of her family, although pride made her reluctant to become a burden on them. But she couldn't run the taverna on her own.

It was Liz who came up with the idea. 'What if I helped to run the business with you. It would really help Yannis and me.' Liz had the expertise, and she and Yannis were looking for somewhere to live. They could move in to the apartment at the taverna in Kalyves and become partners with Eleni.

The elderly woman's eyes were moist with tears. 'That is a kind offer but I cannot let you do that,' a downcast Eleni confided.

'I owe too much back rent on the premises and I couldn't saddle you with the debt. Things have got on top of me recently.'

'Eleni, my daughter,' Vassilis interrupted. 'Perhaps I have a solution to your problem.' All eyes turned to the old man cradling a glass of wine as he listened to the conversation go back and forth. 'You were right to be upset that I have not always provided for the family as I should have. It was not because I didn't care, I felt guilty that I lost everything the family had. I'm so sorry, but maybe this will in some small way go towards making reparation for the past.' The old man pulled a piece of paper from his pocket and handed it to Eleni. I have been waiting for the right moment to give you this. 'Eleni, I love you, I am sorry for the past and although this is little recompense I hope it can make a difference to your future.'

Eleni took one look at the cheque she had been passed by her father and gasped. 'I can't take this, where did you get it?'

In amazement she stared at the figure written on the bank draft. Fifty thousand euros was more money than she had ever had in her life.

'You will take it, what do I need it for, I have everything I could want in life now the family is back together, and it will make me feel better. My obsession with the lyra owes you something, take this at least.'

The old man stood and walked into his workshop and as Eleni stared at the cheque a pair of speakers mounted one either side of the vine-draped pergola sprung to life. The music was unfamiliar, but to the trained ear of Nikos it was unmistakable who was playing the beguiling melody. In the shade of the cottage garden they sat entranced as the sound of Vassilis' lyra painted pictures of the magical island of his birth. The melancholy of its tragic past and the generosity and joy of its indomitable people, it rose to the impossible heights of the tallest mountain peaks and serenely flowed like the deep blue waters of the surrounding seas. Spellbound, when the music came to an end a silent question hung in the air.

'Did you like it?' Vassilis smiled. 'Last year I was approached by a television company in Athens to compose and record the soundtrack for a TV drama, I don't know much about these things but it's one of the biggest ever produced for Greek TV, so I'm told. Anyway, surprisingly they liked what I did. That is the result. You see, music can sometimes pay, it surprised me, even if it is better late than never. When the programme comes out they will release a CD and there might be some more royalties.'

Not for the first time over the last few days the tears streamed down Eleni's lined face. 'Thank you *baba*,' were the only words she could find but they were the only words her father needed. As Sarah blinked away a tear, from the dovecote she saw a pair of doves take wing.

As the coffin was lowered into the concrete-sided grave, through her tears Sarah cast her thoughts back to the day earlier in the year when she had buried her own grandfather; how far she had come since then. Now they were laying to rest his friend and comrade, the man whose bravery had saved John's life all those years before.

It was the following morning they found Vassilis' body. The old man had died in his sleep. As the open coffin lay in the church for the funeral service, Sarah was convinced Nikos' dead *pappous'* face bore a smile. He was carried to the cemetery and they placed flowers on the grave: lilies, poppies and peach blossom.

As the early summer sun beat down, Sarah looked around at the mourners struggling to maintain their composure. Beside her was Nikos, unshaven as is the tradition and wearing a black armband; her mother-in-law Eleni wiped her eyes, head bent in the black dress of a mourning child. Behind them Yannis held Liz's, hand squeezing it tight as he tried to control his emotions.

Exhausted from their sleepless vigil, the mourners gazed out to the Lefka Ori. The white peaks of the mountain range towered above the small group gathered to mourn a man who had changed all their lives in the most profound ways. Through her tears, Sarah thought of how the lyra that Vassilis had lovingly crafted and given to John had indirectly led her to Crete and to find the man she loved and how, in the last few days of his life, Vassilis had found reconciliation with his daughter and set the lives of her friends Liz and Yannis on a new course.

As the casket was committed to the earth, she felt warm gratitude that Vassilis and her own granddad had been a part of her life and enriched it. What they had given Sarah would shape her forever. She looked around at the mountains, then to the deep blue of the Aegean Sea sparkling in the distance before her glance settled on Nikos, and she said a prayer of thanks for the two men who had framed her destiny.

The *makaria* meal after the burial was held in the village taverna, where just a few days before Sarah and Nikos had celebrated their wedding. Little more than three months earlier, Sarah's life had been mapped out in her chosen direction. Those plans had long been buried, like the two men who had since had such a profound influence on her life. On arriving at the taverna the mourners were offered brandy and paximathia, dried bread softened with water with olive oil drizzled over it before a meal of sea bass baked in the oven.

Sitting at the long table, Nikos found comfort in the family and friends that surrounded him. Beneath the table Sarah reached for his hand and he turned to put a consoling arm around his mother. The mood could not stay sombre for long as Sarah joined Nikos and Yannis playing their lyras in celebration of Vassilis' life. For them, with his passing, the circle had been closed. As raki arrived at the table Nikos raised a glass.

'*Eleftheria y thanatos*. Freedom or death.'

Did You Enjoy this Book?

If you liked reading this book and have time, any review on www.amazon.com or amazon.co.uk would be appreciated. My website *Notes from Greece* is at https://notesfromgreece.com, and it would be good to meet up with any readers on my facebook page at www.facebook.com/richardclarkbooks.

Printed in Great Britain
by Amazon